Sex, Sexuality and the Autism Spectrum

also by Wendy Lawson

Life Behind Glass
A Personal Account of Autism Spectrum Disorder
Wendy Lawson
Foreword by Patricia Howlin
ISBN 1 85302 911 4

Understanding and Working with the Spectrum of Autism
An Insider's View
Wendy Lawson
Foreword by Margot Prior
ISBN 1 85302 971 8

Build Your Own Life
A Self-Help Guide for Individuals with Asperger Syndrome
Wendy Lawson
Foreword by Dr Dinah Murray
ISBN 1 84310 114 9

of related interest

Asperger's Syndrome and Sexuality
From Adolescence through Adulthood
Isabelle Hénault
Foreword by Tony Attwood
ISBN 1 84310 189 0

Asperger's Syndrome
A Guide for Parents and Professionals
Tony Attwood
Foreword by Lorna Wing
ISBN 1 85302 577 1

An Asperger Marriage
Gisela and Christopher Slater-Walker
Foreword by Tony Attwood
ISBN 1 84310 017 7

Coming Out Asperger
Diagnosis, Disclosure and Self-Confidence
Edited by Dinah Murray
ISBN 1 834310 240 4

Sex, Sexuality and the Autism Spectrum

Wendy Lawson

Jessica Kingsley Publishers
London and Philadelphia

First published in 2005
by Jessica Kingsley Publishers
116 Pentonville Road
London N1 9JB, UK
and
400 Market Street, Suite 400
Philadelphia, PA 19106, USA

www.jkp.com

Library of Congress Cataloging in Publication Data
Lawson, Wendy, 1952-
    Sex, sexuality and the autism spectrum / Wendy Lawson ; foreword by Glenys Jones.— 1st American pbk. ed.
        p. cm.
    Includes bibliographical references and index.
    ISBN 1-84310-284-6 (pbk.)
    1. Autism—Patients—Sexual behavior. I. Title.
    RC553.A88L392 2005
    362.196'8583—dc22

                                          2004019613

British Library Cataloguing in Publication Data
A CIP catalogue record for this book is available from the British Library

ISBN-13: 978 1 84310 284 7
ISBN-10: 1 84310 284 6

Printed and Bound in Great Britain by
Athenaeum Press, Gateshead, Tyne and Wear

Contents

Foreword by Glenys Jones   7

Acknowledgements   11

Introduction   13

1. Foundations of Who We Are: ASD and
   Sexuality   17

2. Sex Education   31

3. Discovering Relationships   43

4. Being in a Partnership   63

5. Discovering Bisexuality, Homosexuality or
   Transgender Dispositions   81

6. Making It Work   93

7. Building a Safe Place   105

8. Maintaining Our Safe Place   115

9. Accepting and Celebrating Who I Am   129

Appendix 1: Couple Activities Just for Fun   147
Appendix 2: Worksheets   153
Appendix 3: Ben Roe's Sexual Orientation
            Worksheet   159
Appendix 4: A Sensory Profile Discussion Sheet   165
References   167
Further Reading and Resources   169
Subject Index   171
Author Index   175

Foreword

Wendy Lawson has an amazing gift and ability not only to explain how she experiences the world, but then to use this insight and knowledge to help others better understand themselves. She generously shares her personal experiences and shows how her understanding has developed. Despite some very painful and difficult times, Wendy chooses to focus on the positives and explains the strategies she has developed to enhance her personal and sexual relationships.

Little has been written on relationships and sexuality within the context of autism and, as Wendy points out, the literature that does exist is often negative and focuses on the problems that may occur. There are even those who have suggested that it is not necessary or appropriate to provide sex education for individuals with autism. However, as Heta Pukki (2003), a woman with autism, suggests, for some individuals with autism, 'nothing happening' can be as depressing and damaging as an abusive experience and Pukki argues strongly for education on sexuality and relationships. This book will greatly help individuals with autism as it provides clear advice and guidance on how to assess and respond to the behaviour of others. It provides a positive view and will raise awareness amongst professionals and parents of the need to consider and discuss relationships and sexuality.

Wendy's life to date equips her extremely well to write on this topic. She was married for 20 years, had four children, and is now in a lesbian relationship with a longstanding friend. Wendy draws on these experiences and the discussions she has had with her relatives, friends and partners to raise issues and to illustrate useful strategies for negotiating the very difficult territory of gaining and maintaining enjoyable relationships. She uses her own beautifully crafted poems and metaphors to highlight key themes and emotions.

A central tenet of the book is that each person needs first to understand and respect themselves and their own needs, in order then to successfully negotiate how they might relate to others and achieve interdependence. They will need the support, respect and appropriate responses from others to achieve this. This book will be a valuable tool for both those with autism and neuro-typicals (NTs). Wendy describes how in her early life she was confused, depressed, abused and misled by others. Her understanding of how she should be and her ability to read the intentions of others was very limited. She has experienced much rejection, hurt and disappointment in her life, and describes how it is important to move on from these incidents and not to hold grudges against those who have done harm, as this often intensifies and prolongs the pain. She offers useful advice and strategies on how to deal with such experiences. In addition, taking the phrase 'no pain, no gain', she suggests that perhaps difficult experiences and episodes in life can provide material for personal growth, like waste from the kitchen becomes compost for the garden. Wendy recommends that individuals take time out alone on walks or in the bathroom – to reflect on how they feel about the paths their lives are taking, in relation to family and friends. She advocates that individuals take control and responsibility themselves to move in a positive direction and recommends discussing aspects of relationships which are difficult and frustrating either with the person concerned or with a trusted family member or friend.

Neuro-typicals, like myself, who have learned about autism from the outside, frequently read that those with autism have great difficulty in understanding and knowing what it is they need to do or to say in social situations and that they lack social empathy. Such literature can give the impression that NTs are always socially confident and wise. Books like this one, by Wendy, however, demonstrate categorically that those with autism can and do develop social understanding. They also make us NTs question how well we understand, navigate and manage our own personal relationships. Perhaps because individuals with autism have to work out consciously and scientifically what is appropriate, they develop more insight than the

NTs who do not have to consciously pay such attention to this. Wendy argues that she *does* have empathy, but only for things with which she has a connection or attachment. That is, if she has experienced a similar emotion, pain or interest, then she can identify with and share this with another person. From both her positive and her often very negative and difficult experiences in life, together with discussions with those whom she trusts and feels comfortable with, she has developed great insight into how to foster positive relationships, what to disclose and when and to whom, and into the often seemingly 'dishonest' social behaviour of NTs who may feel one emotion, but portray another. The book is written in a style that speaks to individuals with autism and it will be a great guide for them. In addition, Wendy has said in her previous books, that other people (i.e. NTs) are her greatest problem, and that changing the response and behaviour of NTs would enhance the quality of her life and others with autism. This excellent book should go some way to achieving this goal too.

Dr Glenys Jones
University of Birmingham
August 2004

Acknowledgements

I'm sitting at my table looking out over a wondrously blue ocean. The sky above it consists of grey clouds tinged with orange, red and gold. It's been a day of storms, wind, rain and sunshine. My life to date has been like that too! There are so many individuals in my life who are like rays of sunshine. They offer me love, support and, especially, their unconditional friendship.

Relationships can be stormy or smooth; mostly they are a mixture of both. I am thankful to all of those individuals who have contributed to my life and are the reason I am who I am today. I want to give special thanks to my partner, Beatrice, without whom I would not have had the good fortune to discover what real intimacy and a real relationship are about. I also want to thank Dinah, for her unconditional friendship and acceptance. It's also to Dinah and Judy that I am grateful for proof-reading this book and for all their helpful suggestions that have given me an ongoing source of relevant information and encouragement.

To Glenys and Elaine, Jill and Janet, Dave Heyne and Dick, Paul Martin, Don and Alan, Lynne Moxon, Vicki Bitsika, Rose and Mick, Dawn and other friends and 'professionals' in the field, a big thank you for sharing ideas and especially your friendship with me. You guys are Family!

I also want to thank Jessica and her team for taking this book on board and making it a reality!

Introduction

Over the centuries much has been written about relationships, love and sexuality, so why write more? I'm writing more because as an adult with an autism spectrum disorder (ASD) I have not found many answers that fit with my experience of relationships and sexuality in any contemporary text. I have had some questions answered and some explanations given, and I'm thankful to those writers for sharing their experiences. This book goes further. As well as dealing with subjects like basic sex education and ASD, it also attempts to discuss the wider issues of interpersonal relationships, same-sex attraction, bisexuality and transgender issues.

In order to write about ASD, sex and sexuality I need to paint a backdrop for you. This will include an outline that portrays some principles about ASD, sexuality and relationships. For example, when it comes to relationships, being an adult with ASD may have many advantages and a few drawbacks. I'll tell you about some of the drawbacks first. The main drawback is the fact that we live in a world that doesn't understand ASD very well, and this translates to all kinds of relational hiccups (interruptions, discord). As individuals with ASD, we will tend towards being single-minded and the use of single, undivided attention (monotropism). Being monotropic in a polytropic world (one where individuals are multi-channelled, multi-tasked and can divide their attention between a number of interests) will pose problems. For those of us with ASD it might mean that all of our attention either goes towards things that interest us, or towards avoiding things that do not, or towards coping with the confusion of coexisting in a world where the rules, rituals and expectations might be too overwhelming. Unfortunately for us, most other individuals we encounter may find our focused ability a bit challenging.

Another drawback, especially when it comes to relating to others, is connected to (or, depending on your viewpoint, not connected to) 'time'. Time is a very difficult concept overall. Telling the time might not be too hard, but appreciating the process of 'timing' can be a really difficult business. I believed that timetables were created for the sole purpose of informing one of the expected 'time' of any 'timetabled' event (this might apply to public transport, air travel, appointments, engagements, puberty, and so on). However, it is my experience that scheduled events, however well planned, programmed and recorded, may actually present quite differently to that on the timetable. Public transport is often delayed or cancelled, people turn up late for appointments and, even after announcing their intended departure, may linger on as if unsure of whether to stay or to go! Is it any wonder then, for those of us on the autistic spectrum, that timing of conversations, expectations, remunerations and celebrations can be awkward, uncomfortable and even painful? I've suggested this might be a drawback because in spite of the common understanding of difficulties with time, many non-autistic (polytropic) or typical individuals still expect the 'timing' of relational and sexual interaction with monotropic individuals to fit into the meeting of 'their' needs, wants and desires. Therefore, understanding, for many, does not equate to acceptance of difference, accommodation of difference and a providing of space for learning about mutuality.

Sometimes it isn't easy to locate the advantages of being autistic, but I reckon there are many. Being single-minded gives us the edge when it comes to focusing upon an area of personal interest. This might allow us to become very good at what we do. We can often be counted upon to be honest, truthful, trustworthy, dependable and uncomplicated. It appears to me, however, that at times our very 'autistic disposition' is the thing that gets us into the most trouble. Take relationships, for example: neurologically typical individuals (NTs for short) are often dishonest (they feel one thing but portray something else), untruthful (they are apt to state or comment in one way, to please or appease another, as opposed to speaking their mind) and, at times, too diplomatic for their own good (they don't object or protest when they should, so as to keep the peace). At times they try so hard to accommodate multiple interests (of self and of others) that they may be left unable to deliver on promises, programmes and potentials. Instead they might be left feeling overworked, hard-done-by and un-appreciated. Unfortunately though, the very qualities I mentioned above (dishonesty, ability to lie and diplomacy) seem to be the foundation for starting and sustaining various types of relationships!

Let me tell you about a situation I encountered when I was a younger adult. I'd been unwell for several days and felt really rotten (crook, awful). I couldn't understand what the other household members were so upset about (I then lived in a shared community house). My friend was sitting up in bed next to me, her arm around my shoulder. So, she was very close to me, so what? She was holding a cold flannel against my forehead and whispering soothing phrases in her broken English. We didn't talk much...her English wasn't good enough. All I wanted was to bury myself in her lap. To have her run her hand through my hair and whisper gentle words of comfort to me. I don't remember ever feeling so drawn to or so comfortable with another human being. I felt loved, cared for and understood. Everyone else kept away. Nobody wanted to catch the flu. Here was this woman I hardly knew taking time to join me in my misery and soothe those aches and pains. The other members of the household thought it was 'a bad idea, Wendy'. 'You are a grown woman with your own family,' the lady of the house said. 'What has that to do with anything?' I thought.

What I was failing to 'get' at that time were the unspoken rules that exist between people. There are rules about relationships – the dos and the don'ts. I was married and I had children. My husband should be comforting me, not some stranger that I happened to feel safe with. Why? Why is it unacceptable to reach out to another (for a particular type of affection) if they are not part of your existing circle of family or friends? I'm not sure that I have the answer yet, but I do know that displays of affection in public places are often frowned upon. I do know that certain expectations exist for certain relation-ships (fidelity in marriage, trust between parents and their children, loyalty between friends, and so on). I think things can get difficult when and if one isn't familiar with the 'rules' or if the goalposts move and the rules change. I also think relationships can be problematic if they are not grounded in mutual understanding, autonomy and respect.

I have often wondered why some people are upset when they en-counter others of the same sex sharing affection. How do we feel about affection in general? Are we relaxed about it, or does it make us uncomfortable? How do we feel when issues about relationships and sexuality come up in conversation? Are we comfortable with our own sexuality? Sexuality is not just about sex. It is about all of who we are, how and what we think, how we relate, our hopes and dreams – it is about being human. This book aims to explore these issues, as well as offering some support for the journey to self-discovery, rewarding relationships and honest sexuality.

CHAPTER 1

Foundations of Who We Are: ASD and Sexuality

My Body

Heads and shoulders, knees and toes, knees and toes,
This is how the saying goes.
But what of pubic hair that grows?
Of penis, vagina, breasts and those?

What of feelings, periods and figures?
Why do we have them?
Is it the same for Jane, Tom and Ben?
Can we identify all of the triggers?

Do I have to go through this?
Could I not just give it a miss?
I was OK before all of these changes,
Now I erupt into multiple rages.

Now I have feelings I didn't feel before.
Now I have times I can't go out the door.
Now I want what I had before,
but also my body desires so much more.

My mind cannot keep up with all of these things,
My head takes me places where my heart rarely sings.
But then what to do and what should I say?
I think it is best if it just all goes away!

The topic of sex education and sexuality for individuals with an autism spectrum disorder (ASD) is a very important one. Becoming a child, then a teenager and finally an adult will take time. There are so many 'tasks' to complete on the way, and it's as if each one builds upon the other.

In the lives of neuro-typical youngsters life appears to be staged. That is, there are many developmental stages to go through and parents can have some idea what to expect. They can even reflect back upon their own growing-up and utilize this understanding to help their own children.

However, what about individuals with ASD? What about young people with Asperger's syndrome? Is it the same for us or is it different? Well the quick answer is yes and no. Yes, we go through all the same stages of physical development and have all the same hormonal changes that neuro-typical individuals experience. However, no, I don't think we experience these in the same way.

For one thing, ASD is a developmental delay. This means that although physical changes may occur at the appropriate chronological age, emotionally and cognitively they might be delayed (Schopler and Mesibov 1993). For example, Moxon (2001, p.153) points out: '…a strong attachment to, or sexual interest in, someone often occurs later than usual, with adolescent qualities extending well into the person's twenties. Thus emotional changes of adolescence are often delayed and prolonged.'

So this might mean a young teenage boy with ASD may be going through puberty physically, but emotionally or cognitively this boy may be functioning closer to the age of a much younger child. A young teenage girl with ASD may have begun menstruation; having her period means she is physiologically able to become pregnant. However, some young women with ASD of childbearing age may be closer in emotional development to much younger children. Then there are those of us with ASD or Asperger's syndrome who are physically and cognitively equipped for the changes that are happening to us but who lack the 'know-how' of developing and maintaining friendships. We struggle with the 'nitty-gritty' of interpersonal relationships and are disadvantaged in a world that doesn't allow for difference. 'The overriding problem facing people with ASD and

Asperger syndrome – especially in relation to sexuality – is their general difficulty in making, maintaining and understanding social relationships, whatever the person's academic achievement' (Moxon 2000, p.27).

Some of us try really hard to get it right. We might watch other people and try to be like them. We might make attempts at forming friendships but, although many of us desire a friend we are unsure how to go about it. Chartered psychologist Lynne Moxon noted to me in correspondence:

> gay students pick up information from very camp TV performers and are upset when they are rejected by ordinary gays who find their behaviour too bizarre. Sex education is really about relationships and socio-sexual skills... Many individuals with ASD have never had a friend, they have never been to sleep-over or been invited to parties or just out to the cinema with a group of mates.

Then there are those of us who want a romantic relationship but again the social skills needed to know the where, how and when to do and say the right things seem to elude us. Lynne Moxon suggests that the way to help ASD individuals understand better is to begin with teaching about friendship.

> Many of the young men want a girlfriend but do not have the remotest of ideas about what they would do if a girl said she would go out with them. When new students come in September we often have 'engagements' by half term but 'going out with' just means talking at break time or going down to the shop together. Our students learn to go to the pub, to chat; they are good at Karaoke and are great Salsa dancers! From this base they learn that what is important about friends is enjoying yourself with others. From this they can move on to enjoying being with others in a more intense relationship.

So what exactly is 'sexuality'?

According to my psychology dictionary, sexuality means: 'all those aspects of one's constitution and one's behaviour that are related to sex'. Or, sexuality spans the biological, psychological, social, emotional and value dimensions of our lives. Sexuality begins with ourselves and extends to our relationships with others: how we feel about ourselves, as individuals, as sexual beings, how we feel about gender, our body, sexual activity and behaviour. Our relationships with others may include friendship, emotional intimacy, love and sexual activities. We are all sexual beings, regardless of ability, disability or illness, and we have a right to live a fully sexual and satisfying life.

When you understand that sexuality is about *all* of who I am and *all* of who you are, this makes lots of sense. The breakdown of the term 'sexuality' reads like this: SEX U AL ITY. Another way of saying this is: SEX is for U and SEX is for AL(L). The 'ITY' bit reminds me of words like 'entire...ity, un...ity, and conform...ity. I don't have any difficulties with entirety, or with unity, it's the 'conformity' bit that gets me!

The 'rights' relevant to normalization of sexuality for adults with a learning disability are set out by Ann Croft (cited in Mortlock 1993):

1. The right to receive training in social-sexual behaviour that will open doors for social contact with people in the community.

2. The right to all the knowledge about sexuality that they can comprehend.

3. The right to enjoy love and to be loved by the opposite sex, including sexual fulfilment.

4. The right for the opportunity to express sexual impulses in the same form that are socially acceptable for others.

5. The right to birth control services which are specialised to meet their needs.

6. The right to marry.

7. The right to have a voice in whether to have children.

To appreciate how to negotiate these rights and develop an understanding that fosters who we each are as individuals takes specific understanding of processes inherent within our learning styles, which differ according to whether we are neuro-typical or on the autism spectrum.

Typical and atypical learning styles

The learning styles that separate us as either an individual with ASD or an individual with neuro-typicality can be summarized under the following headings. Understanding *polytropism* and *monotropism* (Murray 1992) is primary to who we are and, therefore, to our sexuality. I don't believe we can look at understanding sexuality and ASD without recognizing the differing way we each process life experience. To explore these differences in learning styles in more detail I recommend reading my earlier books (Lawson 2001; Lawson 2003).

Polytropic learning style

Polytropic or neuro-typical (non-autistic) cognitive experience is informed by multi-channelling or polytropism (having several simultaneous interests, e.g. able to integrate visual and auditory channels, or being able to be aware of another's perspective whilst retaining one's own). Polytropic people can look at someone who is speaking whilst listening to them and remain aware of the bigger world both within themselves and around themselves. Polytropism has an impact on all of the following:

- *Non-literality.* Understanding incomplete sentences, incomplete concepts, metaphor and the non-literal 'sense' of everyday life. The ability ro read a person's intention, the context and the scale of the event (overall interpretation).

- *Thinking in open pictures or open concepts.* This means being able to connect experiences, often visually, in an open and continuous manner. This process informs awareness, aids the understanding of social cueing, helps with the sorting of priorities and appropriateness.

- *Social priorities.* For example, social norms, rules, expectations and being sociable, are seen as a priority. Helps with collating information about self, others and society. A useful tool in social relating.

- *Generalized learning.* Having the ability to transfer skills, knowledge and social understanding across differing situations.

- *Few issues with time and motion.* The appreciation of length of time, timing and sequencing. Ability to negotiate stairs, personal space, crowds, emotions, relationships, and so on.

- *Few issues with consequences.* The ability to understand and predict outcomes. Therefore, one can cope with the concept of change, tends not to be obsessive and is more able to move on in one's interpersonal relationships.

- *Possession of a 'theory of mind'.* An understanding of the concept of 'other'. Therefore, one accepts that the 'other' will be different to 'self', with own values, thoughts, beliefs, needs, wants, desires and interests.

Monotropic learning style

Monotropism, having a restricted area of interest aroused at one time, or at its most extreme being singly channelled, means only being able to focus on whatever is in one's current attention tunnel. It can mean only being comfortable with using one channel at any one time, such as the visual channel. Attending to more than one thing at any one time (unless within one's attentional tunnel already) such as looking at someone and listening to them could be difficult. Monotropism will influence the perception of individuals. Individuals with ASD who are not connecting to 'the bigger picture', whether in conversation, understanding or action, might be perceived as being 'rude', not interested or not interesting. This can be a negative when it comes to social relationships, but very much a positive where the role of concentration might be a plus. Monotropism has an impact on all of the following:

- *Literality (or taking things literally).* This applies to sentences, concepts, metaphors, similes, words, expressions, situations and people. For example, not picking up on sarcasm; not 'getting the joke'; only seeing the literal value of words. As a youngster the doctor told me 'hop up on the couch for a minute whilst I talk to Mum'. I timed myself and after exactly one minute of hopping on the couch I told the doctor that his time was up!

- *Thinking in closed concepts or pictures.* For example, having one aspect of an understanding that may be literal, incomplete and in a box all on its own. This may mean not connecting ideas or concepts to other concepts. Not being privy to the 'whole picture' but only getting bits of it can be rather limiting. Within a social context this makes it hard to 'read' others, anticipate their needs, be spontaneous, work or relate without schedules, and refocus after being interrupted.

- *Understanding governed by non-social priorities.* For example, preferred clothing versus fashion; own interest versus interests of others; own feelings and non-appreciation/ understanding of what others feel. This can cause a conflict of interest. Individuals with ASD may not be concerned with appearance, hygiene, being on time, having a tidy home, *or,* quite the opposite, will be regimented about these things to the point of distraction!

- *Non-generalized learning.* This implies not transferring skills or knowledge appropriately across differing domains. May mean applying one general concept of one's beliefs, attitudes and thinking in an inappropriate or over-generalized way to all things. An extension of being literal and monotropic. For example, individuals with ASD might not learn from mistakes, might only apply learning to a specific situation. Not generalizing makes it difficult to differentiate between appropriateness and being inappropriate. For example, teaching that masturbation can occur in the bedroom or the toilet doesn't teach that an individual doesn't need to masturbate every time they go to their bedroom or use the toilet.

- *Issues with predicting outcomes.* For example, not learning from experience or being able to forward-think and work out conclusions. This will mean missing social cues. If one does not comprehend the importance of societal expectation (manners, propriety, timing, sensitivity to 'other', and so on) one might present to others as stubborn, difficult, inappropriate or insensitive. Within the realm of sexuality this can mean social concepts such as being prompt, being organized, being apt, being appropriate in conversation and being generally coordinated are difficult. One might not comprehend the importance of 'special occasions', finding the idea of 'romance' interesting but not necessary, and so on.

- *Issues with 'theory of mind'.* Lack of understanding of the concept of 'other' – empathy lacks and empathy gaps.

The above outline of 'difference' between us as ASD individuals and those who are NT is only a brief guide. It needs to be understood in relation to personality, education, gender, age, belief system, values and experience.

More about ASD and monotropism

So often I read or hear points of view that associate being a neurologically typical person (an NT) with being 'normal' and being autistic as being abnormal. The real issue is with the idea that there is something wrong with not being 'normal' when all normality means is being typical of some arbitrarily identified statistical population. Having ASD might mean we are not in the majority, and being monotropic can cause developmental delays, but it also implies learning is more interesting for us all. There appears to be a long history of specific concerns for individuals with ASD that include being resistant to change and often obsessive (Asperger 1944). I know that this is true for me and has caused me much frustration. However, I sincerely believe that I am more than the sum of my need for structure and my ability to stay focused.

Being an individual with ASD will mean we are differently-abled (we have a 'diffability'). This will mean those of us who are ASD may understand and do things differently to lots of others. The terms ASD and abnormal are no more synonymous than normality is to liking ice-cream! However, I think this is the basis for much of our relational difficulty. Due to our being single-minded, our focus will be like that of a narrow beam of light: we see less of the wider picture. NT individuals operate like a wide beam of light, which allows them to take in more information, even when it is outside of their personal interests. The difficulties come when they have one picture and we have another!

Learning difficulties and ASD

ASD is often accompanied with various learning difficulties. There are those who believe that if you have learning difficulties you will also have limited ability with regard to employment and relationships. I don't think that this has to be a foregone conclusion. In fact it's a very narrow perspective that shows lots of ignorance. Being dyslexic, having an attention deficit disorder with hyperactivity and lots of problems with 'adding up', I know how scatty, disorganized, forgetful and chaotic I can be. So, I need to explore ways that will assist me in the positive development of my own personhood and in the ongoing maintenance of those relationships that are important to me. Our lives can be an interesting tapestry of inviting colour, texture and form that allows the dark threads of difficulty to highlight the golden threads of success. We all need the times of failure in our lives or we couldn't appreciate achievement. At times my inability to 'get things right' really frustrates and annoys me. But my friends tell me that such times are common to us all, and it's better to home in on the things we do get right, allowing opportunity for the other times to diminish, than to fill our minds with failure. It could be said that focusing on mistakes, mishaps and missed opportunities only creates more of the same.

Intellectual disability and ASD

Although intellectual disability and ASD frequently co-occur, they are not the same. The question here is, what equals intellectual disability? For example, I am supposed to have an IQ of 83. I believe that ASD might actually mask some of the real abilities many of us have. The other thing that happens is that, due to our differing learning style, standard IQ tests don't suit us. With this in mind it is important fully to understand intellectual disability and ASD quite separately. Some believe that the lack of spoken language in some people with ASD will mean that an individual lacks the power of thought. This is a myth! Spoken language has certain properties that suggest communication between individuals will be easier. Unfortunately, this does not always bear much relationship to true-life experiences. Even those who have the power of language may not always use it wisely. Words can be used to destroy the reputation of another, they can be used to misguide, misdirect, misinform and harm. They can also be used constructively to build and support a reputation, to offer guidance and direction, and give helpful information. 'Sticks and stones will break my bones but words will never hurt me' is a saying that I always had problems with! Our minds are designed to work with words, images and concepts. In developing concepts, with or without words, we can develop our understanding of self and of other, thus enhancing the chances of success with any relationship.

The term 'intellectual disability' conjures up some very bad vibes for me. This is partly because I was said to be 'educationally subnormal' as a child. It's also because recently I was at a conference where a well-known professor from a well-known university was talking about ASD and genetics and he implied that the time was close when with an understanding of the genetic makeup of ASD and the knowledge of which genes did what, genetic counselling would be available giving parents choices such as abortion or embryo selection. The gentleman then said that some individuals with high-functioning ASD or Asperger's syndrome could lead fulfilling lives and contribute to society. By definition he was implying that those individuals with poor language or no language ability were unable to contribute positively to society. I felt a deep sadness and anger well up within me. I thought about the children and grown-ups I know who, in spite of not talking, find the courage and strength needed for them to face each day. Who, by nature of being human beings, have intrinsic value. Where does the notion that 'one must fit a particular profile to be an acceptable person' come from? It seems reminiscent of a past era that most of us would denounce!

The term 'intellectually disabled' seems to have replaced the term 'retarded'. Actually, retarded more accurately portrays the person's situation. It means a person needs to process things more slowly to make sense of them. It implies the need for others to slow things down a bit, be more patient and give someone more time. Intellectual disability might sound more sophisticated, but does the term remove the individual from 'humanness'? It seems to be something that we commonly do. We take words that somehow make us feel responsible and change them so we are not responsible any more. For example, starting from the benign and moving towards the destructive, 'directionally challenged' means 'I have difficulties reading maps'; 'therapeutic level' means 'give the maximum dose of a drug to keep the drug companies in pocket'; 'mass murder' has become 'ethnic cleansing'; 'intellectually disabled' implies the individual is not quite a 'whole' person. It seems to me that most of us are afraid of what we don't understand, so we try to clothe our fears with terminology that alienates us from facing our fears. This way we can push all responsibility away from self and onto 'other'.

Sex and ASD

Sex and sexuality conjure up certain images that cause discomfort for some of us; however, these are topics that we all need to know about, talk about and understand. Apparently, these topics are the most interesting for us as mortal beings and many hours of internet time are taken up by individuals 'surfing the net' to explore them. Being autistic will not stop an individual from developing sexually or from wanting to explore their sexuality. How they do this though could mean the difference between a useful experience – one that might lead to building good self-confidence – and sad encounters that only unlock the door to low self-confidence, anxiety, depression and even self-injury.

I was once at a conference where a well-known and respected speaker announced: 'Sexuality is not a problem for individuals with ASD. They don't seem aware of their sexuality. If sexuality does present a difficulty then the best thing to do is to redirect the individual... Keep them busy.' I felt really angry when I heard these words. 'Actually, I am a sexual person too,' I wanted to say. 'I have the right to be a sexual person, just like you do,' my thoughts continued. 'Being autistic does not negate our sexuality, it just makes it all a bit more interesting!' I thought. Fortunately, the other speakers at this conference did not hold the previous speaker's viewpoint and quite diplomatically were able to echo the things I was thinking.

As an ASD individual I certainly experience sexual arousal, and knowing what my options are as I explore what to do about this aspect of my identity has been very helpful. I have had the opportunity to ask a number of my friends what they think the issues are for those of us with ASD. All were in agreement that the issues for each of us are similar but in reality the understanding of them will be different.

In a personal communication in response to some questions from me, my friend Dinah Murray said the following about her understanding of sexuality and ASD.

I think the issues are:

Do autistic people experience feelings of sexual arousal?
The answer is: a high proportion do, some of whom also experience sexual satisfaction.

Do autistic people experience feelings of love?
The answer that I can give from my experience is many autistic people – at all levels of apparent ability – feel very strong desire to spend time in certain people's presence, shown by their repeatedly choosing to do so. AND will act to prevent harm to another if they perceive the likelihood of harm.

The whole self/other game being different might mean that the experience of love will be in some ways atypical [as well as all emotional experience being MORE intense]. For some, love as emotion from an Other can be absolutely horrifying; for others it might not make any impression at all.

Love?
But love as *wanting-to-be-with* and *wanting-good-for* is to my mind the core. NT people are generally pretty good at tuning their

emotional states and levels to other people who are good at tuning their emotional states and levels (good shoalers or good at going with the tide).

If a person hadn't even noticed that other people have [quasi]independent emotions which may be influenced by their own, then the nature of their love would be unenriched by that knowledge and s/he would not be able to do the *adjustment-to-please* which may be required for the core needs of *being-with and wanting-good-for to be met by an Other*. And this is where acceptance comes in too: because an accepting Other can accept the loving wish and make it true by doing so ('you are good for me. I do want to spend time with you...'). All the showing of attractively presented emotion which accompanies NT-style love, is just extra[neous]: it's not the core...

Difficulties with fantasy and theatrically based imagination could mean that for some individuals with ASD maintaining 'romance' 'motivation' and 'spontaneity' in their relationships will need effort. They might not even notice when it is missing or why it should be useful in the first place. Some individuals with ASD have said that they are visual thinkers and have strong visual imaginations. I believe for many of us this will mean the need to stay focused upon 'reality' based imagined images of 'Other' and possible obsessions with a person, personage and/or aspects of a person. The fact that so many NT people use fetishes, photographs, films, the Internet etc. etc. to flog their imaginations and promote sexual arousal seems to argue against NT imagination being so much more adequate in this specific area...

Another issue is: *Do autistic people fall in love?*
The answer again is, well sometimes they most definitely do...and the very essence of being 'in love' is a monotropic, obsessive concern with one object, which often appears to other people disproportionate. So when an already monotropic person does experience attraction to another it will have at least some of the qualities of the NT experience – unfortunately it is an inherently loopy state. So the scale problem of monotropism may apply alarmingly to a person who has become an Object of love

whether it is an NT or an autistic person having the experience. Only it is likely to be worse in the autistic case when the whole social thing is so baffling and the chances of striking lucky with reciprocation are therefore so much lower… But it can happen…

CHAPTER 2

Sex Education

Sexual awareness and ASD

When I first started researching sexuality and ASD, I found myself becoming quite upset and even angry. Most of the information seemed to be so negative and only focused upon problems. For example, Gillberg (1984) mentions three main problems that are normally encountered in discussions of sexuality among autistic people:

- they have a tendency to masturbate in public

- they demonstrate inappropriate sexual behaviour towards other people

- many use a self-mutilating technique when they masturbate.

Whilst the above are very real issues for concern they fail to recognize the individual's 'normal sexuality' and his or her sexual needs. Other material talked about how to prevent intellectually delayed autistic individuals rubbing up against each other in mutual masturbative activity. One book I looked at suggested that autistic individuals would never marry but were at risk of being abused or of getting pregnant, and that, therefore, it was a shame that legislation prevented the women in this category from being sterilized! This is particularly scandalous when a pregnancy is often the only clue to ongoing sexual abuse.

I suggest that the neuro-typical world would do well to look within their own ranks to prevent their members from misusing their own sexuality before they lay claim to what to do with us! It seems that there have been various programmes, therapies and treatments for individuals with ASD, but little remedy for being neuro-typical!

Surely, sexuality is part of being human and as such should be rightly appropriated by all of us.

Sexuality is composed of a number of facets. We need to consider them all. Within the neuro-typical population it is understood that recognizing one's own sexuality, learning to respect self and others and eventually forming appropriate relationships that allow mutual sexual expression, is a rite of passage. According to Havighurst, cited in Schopler and Mesibov (1993, p.32), to complete this rite of passage one needs to travel through the following developmental tasks:

1. achieve new and more mature relations with peers of both sexes

2. achieve a masculine or feminine social role

3. accept one's physique and body use

4. achieve emotional independence of one's parents

5. achieve assurance of economic independence

6. select and prepare for an occupation

7. prepare for 'couple relating' and possible family life

8. develop intellectual skills and concepts for civic competence

9. desire and achieve socially responsible behaviour

10. acquire a set of values and an ethical system as a guide to behaviour.

I would have to say that as I look at a number of NT individuals in my life I don't think that they knew they should complete these tasks in order to be sexually active! Pukki (2003) suggests:

> There is very little in terms of the positive: what autistic people actually enjoy, and how one might move towards, and also recognize, good experience. Nothing is said about the benefits of sex in releasing physical and mental tension, or improving a person's knowledge of his or her own body. Emotions are handled clearly from a 'deficit' point of view or not at all. For example, the terms 'obsession', 'infatuation' and 'fierce attachment' are used to describe

the behaviours of autistic individuals, never using the terminology generally applied with normal young people, such as 'falling in love' or 'having a crush' on somebody. This seems to imply belief in an inherently inferior or pathological quality in the autistic people's emotions, instead of just immaturity and inexperience compared to same age peers. (p.61)

As individuals with or without ASD we all experience sexual drives, behaviours or feelings which, at some point in our lives, we may need to discuss with someone. The amount of support we need, however, will be different for all of us. Even those of us at the same developmental level will have differing needs. For example, one person might need to talk about masturbation and how it fits into their life; another needs to know how to develop and maintain friendships; whilst another might need to undertake a sex education course.

According to Schopler and Mesibov (1993), concerns about sex and ASD appear to be influenced by two things:

- communities fearing the sexuality of individuals with ASD

- people supporting the individual's 'sexual rights'.

I think these 'fears' are still legitimate today, but I think we are also more equipped to understand ASD and its impact upon the individual, the family and society (see Lawson 2001). It is hoped that in today's world of 'individual and corporate rights' sexuality and its rightful, respectful and fullest expression is just as available to any individual with ASD as it is to any neuro-typical individual.

We are assuming that all individuals, whether with ASD or without, would benefit from education and support. This would depend upon their developmental age (remember ASD is a developmental delay), interest, motivation and individual requirements.

Perhaps we are reluctant to provide sex education for individuals with ASD because we are concerned about the potential outcome. In other words, we worry about the implications of people with ASD getting married, having children, being able to parent, and other related issues. I think it would be fair to say that these questions are real and necessary, but they are not the immediate ones. It is important to deal with the 'here and now'. We are here and we are sexual beings, yes, but our experiences and needs change over time. We need to be in tune with what our needs are right now and how they differ for each of us.

A couple of examples

A nine-year-old asks his parents one day, 'Where did I come from?' His parents have been wondering when it would be the right time to talk to him about 'sex'. Determined to be honest and give him the facts, they launch into their fullest version of 'the birds and the bees'. The child's puzzled response to all this was, 'Well, does that mean I come from Melbourne or Sydney?'

Gary Mesibov (2001) tells the story about a high-functioning woman with ASD whom he had been counselling regularly. Apparently she had begun dating a man with ASD and Gary was concerned about her understanding of sex. However, the relationship ended rather suddenly and before Gary had a chance to speak with her. When asked why they were no longer seeing one another her response was, 'Well we had been to the library, had dinner out and had gone to the movies. Therefore, there really wasn't anything left for us to do together so it was time for us to begin dating other people.' Gary remarks that his concerns about her ability to be involved in a relationship with another person or to raise children were way beyond her interest and motivation at the time they were working together.

So what I am saying is, it is important to deal with issues as they arise. If an individual isn't ready for a particular intervention or understanding it isn't any good trying to take them there. However, we still need to be laying the foundations of understanding so that they are ready to receive the building as and when it is needed. Crisis sex education is a bit like shutting the stable door once the horse has bolted! We can be so much more effective if we begin before problems arise.

Approaches to sex education

A systematic process

It is safe to assume that sex education is something that is acquired through a systematic process, just like any other concept or skill. For many of us with ASD, this means that it must be learned in a highly structured, individualized way using concrete strategies whenever possible. In addition, the emphasis on language must be minimal because of the difficulties that many of us have with communication. Quite often visual supports (pictures, photographs, video) are useful aids to our understanding. However, we need to be careful that the emotive components of 'sexuality' don't cloud the overall objective.

I am reminded of one worker who suggested she couldn't work with a particular client any longer because the client was 'too sexual' in front of her. This worker took the client's actions and words personally, though I doubt very much if this was the intention of the individual with ASD. For most of us we react, rather than choose to act. In fact, if you don't give us the tools to choose to act, we can only react! Just like NT individuals I am driven by emotions, feelings and (definitely) hormones, but this is only part of the picture. I need information that helps me access the rest of the story. The outcomes of too little information and incomplete concepts can mean that I say and do things that might embarrass others. This is not my intention, I just may not realize how other people will be affected by my literal and incomplete understanding. If I don't access the appropriate understanding, I may just be the product of my feelings.

To put it bluntly, sex education for children with ASD needs to be taught as other things are taught. It will involve many of the same techniques as teaching sorting, matching, letter identification, and the many other skills that have much less of an emotional outcome.

Although sex education must be taught as one teaches other skills, there are also some differences in terms of the priorities we attach to sexual behaviour and our tolerance for deviance in this area. Life is full of incomplete concepts and, as individuals with ASD, we need others to complete them for us. Whether the concept is about drying oneself after a shower, buying appropriate groceries from the shop, knowing what it means when the bell goes for end of class, or the art of sexual intercourse, they are not seen as being any different for us. Therefore, it is important that the gaps are filled, the concepts completed. There may be a wide range of behaviours that are 'allowed' for us – that we can 'get away with' – but this is not the case with sexual behaviours.

Society doesn't take too kindly to individuals who 'let it all hang out'. It might be that an individual is only unzipping their pants in preparation for going to the bathroom, but this might not be understood by the general population. Therefore, teaching full and appropriate concepts about sexuality is very important.

A developmental approach

Having a developmental approach is essential. We all develop at different rates and in different ways. It is important to take things in small steps, to start at the beginning and at an appropriate place, and to move through the events in sequence and only give as much information as is appropriate. As the individual achieves all of the skills related to a specific level, that individual is then ready to move on to higher skills and concepts.

No two individuals are the same. You need to use different techniques and strategies for differing levels of learning, skill and understanding. For example, a person without verbal language and a measured IQ below 25 will require very different sex education programmes from one who is verbal with a measured IQ around 100 or above. When one is engaged in sex education one also needs to consider realistic long-range goals. I know one young man who says he will marry at 20, live in the country and have one girl and one boy. I don't think that this young man really has an understanding of his 'goals'. Just because someone is verbal we shouldn't assume they have the understanding to match their words!

Considering the developmental age of an individual with ASD should also guide our conversation. The impulsiveness, aggressiveness, confusion and defiance that often accompany the biological and physical changes occurring in adolescents with ASD are often not so different from those same behaviours occurring during normal adolescent development.

All sex education must consider the communication level, social skills, cognitive ability, conceptual ability, and all other aspects of a person's functioning. For example, two adolescents with ASD might have the same general IQ and language ability but very different interpersonal experiences. If both express a desire to date, then their sex education programmes would have to differ accordingly. The individual who isn't too good at understanding the concepts of 'friend' or 'romantic attachment' might have to focus on some simple interpersonal skills, such as looking at other people, initiating conversations, and developing appropriate interpersonal strategies. Dating might still be an appropriate long-range goal, but this would be much further down the line. On the other hand, a young adult who has already mastered these skills would be able to focus on applying them in an interpersonal setting. This person's programme might be based more on understanding interpersonal needs, what people do on dates, handling sexual issues, and other related concerns. Although these adolescents may be approximately the same age and have similar cognitive and communication skills, their social development would dictate different teaching strategies.

TEACCH

According to the TEACCH programme (see www.teacch.com) there are four levels of sex education:

- discriminative learning (what to do where, when and how, etc.)

- personal hygiene (where, how often, changing underwear, etc.)

- body parts and functions (sex organs, male and female roles)

- sex education programme (from friendships to sexual intimacy).

DISCRIMINATIVE LEARNING

The most basic sexuality skills that all individuals with ASD must learn are simple discrimination skills. These include knowing when and where to undress, masturbate, touch other people, and all other related behaviours. For individuals with ASD who have little language and are functioning at the severely monotropic end of the spectrum, this might be all they are able to achieve in the area of sex education. However, mastering this understanding will be vital to the success of everyday life within any community.

As with the teaching of any other skill, sex education is best based upon rewarding and reinforcing desired outcomes rather than on saying 'No', as well as providing consistency and structure. For example, as well as rewarding appropriate behaviour, stop signs for 'out of bounds' places to masturbate can be useful along with green 'Go' signs for where it is OK, for example, the individual's bedroom. Please remember, though, that it needs to be made clear that only these signs are for this purpose as opposed to go and stop signs elsewhere! If the individual wants to work out other signs that they prefer, this should be encouraged.

Discrimination training can be facilitated by environmental manipulations that make desired behaviours more likely and undesirable behaviours more difficult to perform, for example, the wearing of a belt, making it more difficult to put hands in pants, the wearing of tops without buttons, zips at the back, and so on.

I can be oblivious to others whilst at the same time totally switched on to my own 'needs'. One lad I knew, when he was young, would lie on the couch with his hands in his pants, his T-shirt over his head... to his way of thinking, we couldn't see him! I can think of a young man who regularly removed his clothing en route to the bathroom. He thinks 'need to go to the bathroom, toilet' and begins the process of getting ready. I would suggest that monotropism, being singly minded, plays a role in this.

PERSONAL HYGIENE

Personal hygiene doesn't only affect us, but impacts upon others too. It is something that ensures personal comfort and the comfort of others around us. Understanding in this area will include cleaning oneself properly after using the toilet, appropriate hygiene during menstruation, changing underwear, cleaning oneself appropriately in a bath or shower, possibly using deodorant, and other related behaviours.

BODY PARTS AND THEIR FUNCTION

There are a number of good books that are available to help parents impart understanding of how our bodies work. I like this part very much. My hunger for facts and information makes this bit not too difficult. What teachers need to do though is check in on our understanding. Knowing all the right terms, and being able to spout out what they mean or what they do, does not equate to understanding appropriateness and propriety.

Complete sex education

More and more individuals with ASD are keen to relate sexually to others and some of us are interested in long-term relationships. Having the knowledge and support that enables us to choose what we want to do with our lives and futures is vital if we are to choose wisely.

WHO CAN PROVIDE SEX EDUCATION?

Finding out about sex and relationships is an ongoing discovery. Initially, sex education might be taught by our parents; they might talk to us, explore written material on the subject, help us learn through caring for pets and so on. Sex education might be part of the school curriculum, so school teachers will guide us into an appropriate understanding. For some of us it's what we learn from our peers that has the most impact. Learning about sex and sexuality should never be forced upon us and we should not consent to behaviour we are not comfortable with.

There is lots of information about sex, even if there is no one available to talk to, but it's important to get the right kind of information; not all information about sex is right for everyone. For example, there are many good books – see the list at the end of this book. There are also some good therapists and sex educators: often local community centres give addresses of qualified individuals.

Some related issues

Same-sex affection

What is same-sex love? Why does it cause the hairs on the back of the neck to bristle up and give a sense of fear to some? One might comment, 'Well, it's unnatural, ungodly and perverse.' Is it? I remember being told, 'But even the bible says it's wrong to leave what is natural for that which is unnatural.' This begs the response, though: 'That which is "natural" to you might not be "natural" for others and vice versa.' Why does society choose to believe that everyone is the same? Some individuals are not heterosexual. If some individuals are not naturally heterosexual, then it follows that they are not going against 'nature', rather, being homosexual or even bisexual is natural to them. It is worth noting that same-sex sexual interaction frequently occurs in the animal world. Could it be that they are less inhibited than we are?

So, what might it mean for relationships if one is only attracted to members of the same sex? What might it mean to feel same-sex love and be autistic? It will mean different things to different individuals, but it is a valid orientation and needs positive consideration. I write more about same-sex attraction, from a personal perspective, later on in this book.

Over-attachment

At times, when one reads about ASD, some literature states that individuals with ASD are not good at forming attachments to humans. It is important to state here that children with ASD form attachment to parents just like NT children do, there isn't any difference. There is also the idea that in ASD individuals attach more readily to 'objects' rather than to other people. This seems to be true for some. However, one of the things that caused me the most discomfort and difficulty in my past relationships, was my 'over-attachment' to individuals of the same sex. Attachment is normal and healthy, when it is balanced (not obsessive), reciprocated and rewarding. It has taken me a very long time to work this out and I will write more about this later on in this book.

Role-play

I think that when it comes to relating to anyone at any level, after reading the books, watching the videos and engaging in conversation, *appropriate* role-play can be useful. Role-play is like putting the final bricks in the wall – the top layer that completes the building. For this level of understanding to register, a significant amount of role-playing is needed. As in many areas, we, as individuals with ASD, have difficulty learning when we are only given a verbal instruction, we tend to need much more concrete information. Role-playing creates a more concrete setting and enhances our learning. Therefore, role-playing how to meet other people, how to talk to them, how to deal with problems that occur, is an important part of learning about relationships. Role-playing helps to make some of the more obscure concepts easier to understand and use. So, role-playing is another tool that, used wisely and not inappropriately, can help us access and implement a wider understanding.

Noticing others

I well remember a friend's 40th birthday. There were 23 people at my friend's birthday party. I don't usually 'do' parties. If I do venture into such an event I usually give the birthday person their birthday present, say 'hello' to the other early arrivals like myself, then leave. At this party I had tried to stay on a bit longer. Mostly I had managed because I took on the role of chief waitress and dish-washer. Hiding in the kitchen when I wasn't collecting plates and glasses gave me some personal space to escape the noise and social demand. I found that by taking on this role I could stay longer at such events. This gave me a chance to hear various snippets of conversation and to witness what most people did at group functions. Much of the social interaction didn't make sense to me, but I was intrigued by the behaviour of certain individuals towards other certain individuals. I later came to understand that the behaviour I was witnessing was called 'flirting'.

When I was a child, time and time again, I failed to form any kind of long-term friendship. I didn't want lots of friends, but it would have been nice to have just one. What is the secret ingredient to a 'good' friendship? Now, as an older adult I think that I know the answer. I will attempt to share it with you within the pages of this book.

CHAPTER 3

Discovering Relationships

Relationships

I didn't choose my parents and they did not choose me.
We are quite different people, it's certainly plain to see.
Although we share some common features,
Passed on from them to me,
We are all individuals and different we will be.

Now difference poses problems that arise for one and all.
Some of us are short and some of us are tall.
Some of us like quietness, solitude and all,
Whilst others like it noisy, chaotic and much more.

Relating to others will mean finding common ground.
I need to notice that there's more than me around.
For this to happen with success it takes us both you see,
I need to notice you and you to notice me.

There are degrees of friendship, this is how it should be,
Some people are polite to all but choose more sensibly
Those to spend their time with, those they should ignore,
Those they can work with and those that they adore.

Unfortunately there is no 'one size that fits all',
In fact some will tell you 'all is fair in love and war'.
So if the rules keep changing and people will change too,
How can you relate to me and I relate to you?

The questions I hope to address (outlined below) are taken from a list of questions that came up at a camp I attended for individuals with ASD. I will also explore questions under specific headings as the book continues.

- How do I know if I am attracted to someone; if the attraction is appropriate; if the attraction is mutual; and what to do about it?

- Sex and relationships sound like good things but what are they actually for?

- Is having a relationship worth all the trouble it may cause?

- Should grown-ups with ASD be responsible for their own love life?

- Should parents, friends or carers have any rights to make decisions on behalf of the individual with ASD?

- Is there an age of consent for us as individuals with ASD?

- What factors would need to be considered to demonstrate that we have knowledge of right, wrong, appropriateness etc.?

- What are the risks of relating and how do you recognize them? How can I know if someone is just taking advantage of me?

- Do we have a right to not be in a relationship? How do we handle pressure from friends and family? Are our rights clear to us?

How can we learn about all of the above things, practise these or prevent them? I hope that this book, amongst others (e.g. Segar 2001; Newport and Newport 2002) might be helpful. I also hope that we can share our concerns with a good friend or a support person whom we can trust.

A relationship can mean different things to different people. Some relationships are easy and some are difficult. Many relationships exist out of necessity and not choice (e.g. family relationships, work relationships). But, whichever way we look at it, relationships are about convenience, connection, correlation, commitment and community. The subject of this book – human relationships, with particular emphasis upon romantic relationship and partnership – is no different.

It takes two to tango

What are relationships for?

Some would say the idea of relationship came from early scripture when God suggested that it wasn't good to be 'alone'. The concept of two being better than one, in certain situations, was because if one was hurt, had fallen over or was infirm, then the other could assist. Sharing the load and pulling together can make the demands of life less daunting and less difficult. It also provides another person to share your joys with. Of course, there can be good relationships, bad relationships, and those that are indifferent. Some relationships occur because individuals share a common goal. Others are based on financial need, sexual or romantic attraction, needs for security, 'seemed like a good idea at the time', or all of the above.

Whatever the basis for our relationships, to be positive and pleasing they will need to be mutual to some degree. The relationship between parents and their children tends to be heavily weighted towards parents taking the lead, making the major decisions, providing security and giving care to their offspring. It's rather lovely when children recognize parental care, love and sacrifice and can demonstrate their appreciation. However, the responsibility of parenting remains that of the parent until the child grows into an adult and develops the ability for self-care.

Like so many others I have been involved in a number of relationships. Some of those relationships have been very constructive and continue to exert a very positive influence over my daily life. However, there have been some relationships that haven't been positive. They have left me feeling wounded, defeated and battle-scarred. Maybe it's only as we sift through the debris, clutter and mess of various relationships that we eventually understand.

It is important to distinguish between relationships that only cause damage and the general 'ups and downs' that healthy relationships can go through. Because, as human beings, we are all fallible we will experience difficult times in our good relationships – misunderstandings, different ideas and opinions, disagreements, miscommunication and misrepresentation. When these things happen it is a good idea to share our thoughts and feelings with the other person and sort it out before it grows into something ugly. However, even here it is important to tread carefully. How should one 'share' feelings? How do I identify what I feel? How do I sort out what I should say, do or think? When is it the right time to do this? But it needs to be borne in mind that even if we come up with some general rules that have worked for some of us, they may not work for everyone. The best thing is to explore with care and check your life encounters against your own experience, not against that of others. Some things will feel comfortable and sit well with you, others will not. One rule that I tend to follow is *'If in doubt, leave it out.'*

Quite often our parents and siblings can be helpful when it comes to talking about ideas of what relationship means. Our friends will have ideas too, then there are books we can read, like this one.

Do I need other people?

I think that as human beings we are designed to live interdependently. Some of us will need more people in our lives and some of us will need fewer. As a younger person I didn't know how to form friendships or relate appropriately to other people. I either formed over-attachments or no attachments at all. Being monotropic means I'm a kind of 'all-or-nothing' person. In the past this has got me into lots of trouble. I wasn't able to separate 'myself' from 'other'. I couldn't identify the components for a healthy relationship, whether that meant what should come from me or from others. I didn't understand the issues associated with personal space, personal need, personhood or personal worth. Everyday life was so difficult to negotiate that I tended to live it through another. This means that my decisions were not based upon my own understanding but based upon what others told me. It meant not being able to trust my own instincts, desires, ideas or thoughts. I constantly needed to access emotions, activities and thoughts via someone else. This is very tiring for all concerned and yet it has taken me years to understand what was happening and how to mostly avoid it. I definitely still have times when I struggle with this.

What am I responsible for?

Each of us can learn how to identify what is our responsibility and what is not. When I am unsure I can ask myself a set of questions. For example: Is this person an adult? If they are, they are responsible for their decisions, I am not responsible for their choices. I am responsible for my choices though. Did I choose to do, think or feel this? Is the outcome a result of my action? Did I know what was going to happen if I did this? If I did not know then am I responsible for the outcome? I might not be. There are lots and lots of questions that I need to ask myself, and sometimes I need to check in with others too.

In an ideal world once we become adults we are responsible for our own decisions. The difficulty might be that even though we are grown up physically we might not be emotionally mature enough to know if an individual is 'right' for us or not, and we might not recognize if someone is just using or abusing us for their own needs, rather than being considerate of our needs too. If we have a good friend or family member we trust then we should be able to be guided by their advice, because they have our best interests at heart. A good way to check this out is to talk about this and to ask for their opinion. We can also ask for their support in making our decisions.

How do we know if we're ready to build a relationship?

We may not know if we are ready to build a relationship but we might know if we feel interested in relating to or being friendly with someone else. Most relationships begin with mutual interest, and this is a good foundation for building towards a healthy friendship. As we get to know someone and allow him or her to know us, a more romantic relationship might develop. All of this takes time. This is a good thing because it means we don't have to rush into anything we are unsure of.

Dating

Most first dates are full of anticipation and the sense that one wants to 'get it right'. Choosing appropriate clothing (clean, comfy and suited to the occasion) is the first part of this. Taking the time to listen to the other person and not bombard them with questions or with statements about the things that interest us is another component. It takes time and practice to learn how to relax around another person and how to enable the other person to feel at ease with us. So, go slowly and allow the friendship to develop. If, after some time getting to know each other, you or the other person decides not to continue with developing a romantic relationship, this is OK and you can say so. The process of getting to know someone can turn up things about a person that you feel uncomfortable about, or can help you realize you are not suited as a couple. This may happen for the other person too, and they may decide not to continue with you. This is a normal, healthy and usual path to discovering the kind of partner you fit best with.

Do I have to have a boyfriend or girlfriend to be normal?

No, you do not. Lots of individuals do not have a boyfriend or girlfriend and are very happy and healthy people.

What if I'm desperate and I have to have a boy or girlfriend now?

Feelings of desperation can completely dominate our thinking, but we still don't have to allow them to rule our lives. Learning to delay gratification can be a useful tool. Although you might feel that you need a boyfriend or girlfriend NOW, actually you don't. You might like to have one, you might wish you did have one, but this is different to NEEDING one now. You can take time to seek out an appropriate friend and explore where it leads you. You can spend time in other pursuits as well. The more you feed a desire, the more fuel you give it, the more the fire burns. But, if you take the fuel away from that fire it will, eventually, go out. Why allow yourself to be controlled by this feeling? Take time to learn how you can take back the control your life needs, and see where the journey takes you.

How do I deal with people who think I should not have a
relationship?

Whatever we do there will always be an objection raised by someone.
'If we never ever go we will never ever know' is an Australian saying.
If we are keen to pursue a relationship and feel safe and comfortable
to do so, then maybe we should tread gently, go slowly, make no
commitments to anything, but give it a shot! We don't always need
the approval of others. I know many couples who have been together
for years, but whose parents think that the partner of their son or
daughter is not good enough for them.

If, however, the consensus from our family is that we need to wait
a while longer, perhaps until we are older, more mature or until we
have more understanding, then we might need to listen to their advice. We could ask them how we will know when the time is right for
us to pursue a relationship. What signs will they be looking for? They
might even create the information into a chart for us so we can see
ourselves developing towards our goal of being ready for
relationships.

Is there a set of rules for being a friend?

The only rule that I aim to follow is the ancient saying 'Do unto
others as you would have them do unto you.' One can aim to keep the
lines of communication open by being available to talk things over;
be ready to hear the words of others and be prepared to change your
view. I once watched a movie where one character stated, 'From
where I sit you are way over your head.' The other character replied,
'Well you need to change your seat then.' This was a fair comment,
and one I aim to utilize.

Are there some role models that I could copy?

In an ideal world our parents should be our role models. The
difficulty here is that they are human, fallible and have their own
problems. It's not a good idea to copy what we see on the television
either. Some 'soaps' portray 'loving relationships', but to keep us all
watching them they introduce dilemmas and catastrophes that are not
so common in reality. The best thing is to read wisely, talk often and

watch with interest those relationships around us. Then, think about what it might mean for us, in our relationships.

Coping with rejection and disappointment

Rejection and disappointment are painful emotions and really do cause us heaps of discomfort. If the person who has rejected or disappointed us is still around us (a work colleague, a family member) and we have to encounter them frequently, we might need support to get over our pain. Support comes in the form of other people, yes, but it also comes in the shape of our own thinking. For example: 'So what if that person doesn't want to relate to me any more. I'm still an OK person. They are allowed to choose not to relate to me if they want. I can choose not to relate to them. I will be polite but I will use my energy to focus upon other things that interest me. I have more time now to explore my other options too.'

It takes time to recover from a broken relationship and you might find you need time away. Maybe you need a holiday? Maybe you need to spend some time with others whom you can share and relax with?

Freeze framing

'Freeze framing' is a term that comes to mind when we are 'stuck' in an emotion or belief that dominates our thinking so much that the experience is our only frame of reference and it's frozen us in time. I have known this feeling well and it has ruled my life on occasion. Not only is this uncomfortable to those of us who are experiencing it, but it's also uncomfortable for many others around us. We may 'hold a grudge' against someone or 'carry a chip upon our shoulder'. This may be so strong that it dominates not just our thinking but also our conversations and our actions. A few years ago I realized that my anger with a certain individual was actually hurting me. My sense of injustice may or may not have been the whole story, but now, the person concerned didn't even know what was happening to me and even if they had they wouldn't have cared! So, my plots and schemes for punishing them; my anger and pain; the thoughts that tortured me, which led into affecting others; all were wasted! Their only purpose was to keep my pain alive. I realized that by maintaining my anger I was giving 'that person' the power to continue to hurt me. This realization began the process of letting go of my pain and the process of healing was enabled.

Freeze framing doesn't just apply to emotive responses like anger though, it also applies to other emotive states. For example, at times one can find oneself feeling absolutely 'frozen' in a state of panic, apprehension or fear. These emotions may be connected to the presence of another individual or even to the mere mention of their name. I'm not sure why this happens, I just know it does. Perhaps there is a sense that when a particular person appears on the scene, we will not have the control over our emotions that we had before their arrival. It might be that this person stirs attraction in us. It might be that they stir up some kind of expectation or dread that we haven't been able to process and, therefore, we don't know what to do or how to interpret our responses. This state for us is truly uncomfortable and can even cause us to react as if our life were threatened. I wonder if it is this kind of emotion that can precipitate self-injurious behaviour or actual harm to others.

I'm not sure what the answer to freeze framing is, especially when it is triggered by attraction, but I hope that after identifying what might be happening, we can then explore some possibilities to help us work through these awfully difficult responses to arriving at a place where we are back in control and can respond appropriately.

Telling somebody about our diagnosis

When is it the right time to disclose to another person that we are on the autistic spectrum? Although it's difficult to pinpoint the precise time for this to occur there are some principles and signs to guide us. The first question to ask is 'How is this relationship doing?' For example, have we both spent some time together discovering our interests, likes and dislikes, our personalities, and what we hope for in the future? Do we want to continue to develop our relationship? If the answer is 'yes', then are we ready to share about our backgrounds, our families and our learning styles? If the answer to this question is 'yes', then it might be a good time to talk about our diagnosis. It's important to remember that being an ASD person (person with an autistic spectrum diffability) means we have a different learning style to NT individuals. If the person you are building a relationship with is an NT individual, they need to understand your learning style, but you also need to understand theirs. If the person you are relating with is also an ASD person, then even though your learning styles fundamentally may be similar, you will be different people with different experiences, different family background, different personalities and different expectations. These 'differences' will impact upon your relationship and will need to be explored. It won't be necessary to explore them all at once, but the need to acknowledge them is important.

Later on in this book you can read about my experiences as I 'disclosed' to others about my ASD and about my sexual orientation. I was pretty naive about how others would respond and, maybe, I could have done it differently. The reality is that there is no absolutely 'right' way to disclose who we are that will guarantee a positive reaction from other people. Even if we do all the things we believe we should, we cannot be responsible for the other person's response. This doesn't mean, therefore, that we shouldn't tell them; it just means that we need to be prepared for a range of responses, some of which might not be welcome.

Attraction

What does it mean to feel attraction?

How do I know if I am attracted to someone, if the attraction is appropriate, if the attraction is mutual, and what to do about it? How do I let someone know I'd like to date him or her? Attraction between people (interest in them romantically or sexually) is a common feeling and for some people is a frequent occurrence. Physically being 'attracted' to another person might feel uncomfortable. You might feel your heart pounding in your chest and a strange discomfort in your 'tummy'. There might be apprehension and even panic at the thought of encountering 'that person'. These are normal feelings and most people cope with the experience. But for some of us these feelings can rule our lives and completely dominate our time. The 'panic' feeling can be so strong that it immobilizes us. The fear we feel with all of its associated physical reactions can cause huge discomfort and even make us ill. I think that one reason we feel it so strongly is because we are monotropic and all of our attention goes to this one spot, for example 'attraction to this person and fear for what that might mean'. We are also very literal so it's hugely difficult to be open to 'reason', or a variety of reasonable thinking, that might help us to deal with our thinking, for example, 'my feelings are so strong they are my reality, there is nothing else'. Our monotropic thinking only allows us to access part of the picture, though we need to get a bigger picture of what's happening so we can get a more accurate perspective.

So, the first thing is to understand what attraction is, then what it might mean for us, then what, if anything, we can do with it. Understanding that one doesn't need always to act upon this feeling is helpful. That means it's OK to feel this, just like some other feelings that might be uncomfortable, but it might not require action. Usually one needs to check a few things out first. Is this person likely to be available, and if so are they likely to be interested in me or 'right' for me? Once we have answered these questions (e.g. checked out if the attraction is mutual by asking if they want to go out with us) and we feel assured that the other person is available and is interested in relating to us, then we can continue to further the attraction and start to develop a friendship. Quite often the process of getting to know someone will have the affect of 'dimming' the uncomfortable feelings that go with the attraction, and although the excitement may continue, the panic eases.

Liking someone who doesn't like us
Just like you won't like everyone, there will be times when someone doesn't like you. It's really unfortunate if we are really drawn to another individual but they don't fancy us. I know that this is uncomfortable, but we can live with it. One just has to accept that this is how it is sometimes.

How do I understand the signals people give me?

For example, if someone smiles at me, does that mean they want sex with me?

People often smile at one another and it's usually just a form of greeting that is intended to be interpreted as 'hello'. In some environments it might mean more than this, so the way to know is to respond with a smile and nothing more. If the smile was not a simple 'hello', the responsibility to make that clear is upon the other person, not upon you. A good rule of thumb is to respond with the same greeting that was given to you.

Is the attraction mutual?

Liking and wanting to relate to another person is usual and is a common desire for most of us. Although the feeling of being attracted to another person might be uncomfortable, and this discomfort tends to be intense and to dominate our feelings, it is important not to act in haste. We need 'time' to process what's happening to us. An important issue, therefore, is to give ourselves that time.

We might meet someone at our place of employment, education or social gathering who interests us. Our interest might be sparked initially because they smiled and showed friendliness. Or, it might be because during conversation we felt comfortable and 'at home' with this person. Where there is interest and it appears to be mutual, there is a chance for a friendly relationship to develop. Being a friend and building a friendship over time might be the prelude to wanting a deeper relationship with another person. The only way to explore if this interest, is mutual is to enquire of the other individual if they feel the same way. One needs to ask them the question, at the appropriate time (not whilst they are busy or in company with others), whether they would like to go out, to the movies or to dinner perhaps. If it's easier we might like to write a letter to the person concerned, stating our interest, and then we need to wait for their reply. If they do not write back it probably means they are not interested in relating to us. At this point the best thing for us is to respect their decision, even though we might not agree with it, and turn our attention elsewhere. Sometimes individuals are very friendly people and they enjoy our company but they are not interested in developing a deeper or romantic relationship. It might be they already have such a relationship in their lives or it might be that they like us as a friend, but are not interested in us romantically. It's OK for the individual of our interest not to be interested in us and they might say 'no' to our invitation of a date with them. If they say 'yes' though, what should we do next?

If we are in a relationship, what do we do if we feel attraction to somebody else?

Even though we might be developing a relationship based upon mutual attraction it doesn't mean that our feelings will only be inspired by that one individual. This is good news because it means that if our current relationship isn't working, there are opportunities for other relationships. However, sometimes when we feel really good and comfortable with the way our relationship is going, we can still feel drawn to someone else. The rule here is usually that it's OK to feel attracted to another person, even if you are already in a relationship, but although it's OK to feel attracted, it's best not to act on that attraction. This means feelings are OK, and we can't stop them happening; but if we want to maintain our current relationship, that's where our attention and energy need to be focused, not taken up with a different person. Sometimes this means choosing to ignore the feeling and act lovingly towards one's partner instead. Love isn't always a 'feeling'; at times it's a choice when feelings don't figure much in the scenario at all. I think feelings are pretty flimsy things that change like the wind. Loyalty, commitment and care of another show true 'love', and are the basis for the relationship.

Meeting people

Flirting – how the hell do you do it?

Flirting or casually hinting to another individual that they interest you and that you want to know them better can be a risky business. Sometimes it seems easier to do this at social gatherings where people might be more relaxed and there is space and time for this to happen. However, we can give out a signal to someone that is read as a sexual 'come-on' and this might not be what we mean. It is best to be really clear about what we want and to aim to gauge what the other person wants too. I think this can be very difficult! Some people are only interested in the come-on, the flirting. The very act itself is a game that many seem to find enjoyable. The tease is not meant to culminate in any sexual or romantic act, but is just fun in itself. Working all this out is a delicate procedure, and one that many do not master with any great perfection. It is OK to practise this and not to take it too seriously. It seems that typical individuals practise this frequently. In safe places, like 'a good family' (not all families are safe places), little girls flirt with their daddies and even siblings tease each other. This is a common form of 'pretend play' as a way of rehearsing for the real thing. Making mistakes in a safe place is OK, making them in a place that is not so safe, however, can lead to devastating consequences.

Usually flirting consists of smiles and gestures that let another person know you are romantically interested in them. Being coy, shy and playing 'hard to get' are all part of the flirting process. Others use different tactics, however, and can be quite bold in their attempts to portray their romantic interest for the other person. I find the behaviour between birds in the spring-time really humorous and pleasing to watch. For example, the male pigeon will coo, fluff up his feathers and prance around the female hoping to allure her with his qualities. The male robin will sing and puff up his gorgeous crimson breast in his efforts to attract a female robin. All really interesting stuff for the bird world; in the world of humans, however, it is often the female who adorns her person with colourful and alluring attributes in the hope of attracting a mate. One of the best ways of observing 'flirtatious' behaviour amongst humans, with a view to learning how to do it, is to watch television programmes that demonstrate such behaviours. Quite often a love story between people will have highlights of this behaviour and you can watch with interest. One of the rules of flirtatious behaviour, though, is noticing if it's reciprocated or not so that you can decide what, if anything, you need to do about it.

Ordinary nightclubs and pubs – do they work for us?
Pubs and clubs are an acceptable place for meeting others. They are the ideal environment for one to 'let down one's hair' so to speak. The

difficulty might be though that the noise and sounds that contribute to some people's fun might be overwhelming for others and interfere with the processing demands of thought and action. I'm not good with conversation in noisy places. If all my attention is needed to process the act of just being in a pub or club, then it might mean I won't notice the other important aspects of relating to others. For these reasons pubs and clubs might not be the ideal place for individuals with ASD to show off their best side with the aim to attracting a 'date'.

Personal columns

The personal columns are the sections in the paper or magazine where you can place an advertisement to let someone else know you are interested in finding someone to share with. They usually give out information about your gender, age, location, interests, hobbies and best attributes. For example, 'Fun-loving male seeks female to party with. Must have own transport, be between 20 and 30, and live in the London area.'

Personal adverts may be useful for some, but not all of us, depending on our disposition, personality and ability to process the concepts involved. This applies to all individuals, in fact, on the autism spectrum or not.

How can we maximise our chances of getting involved with someone?

It seems to me that the best idea is 'steady as she goes'. This is an expression that means 'don't rush things, go slowly'. Give the relationship time to become established. If another person feels they are being pressured into relating to us, they will feel very uncomfortable and might even decide to back off. Although I think it's a good idea to have a long-term perspective, this needs to unfold bit by bit. If the other person only wants a one-night stand and isn't interested in developing a serious relationship, we need to understand their perspective and check in that we are happy with this too. One-night stands or brief encounters with others can be fun and learning experiences, but we must be sure that this is what we want and not just what the other person wants. We are certainly allowed to say 'no' to any request made of us, and if we are not interested or do not feel comfortable, we should say so.

Nervousness and anxiety

Everyone gets nervous sometimes, it's a common feeling. I try to remind myself that if I am nervous around another person they might be feeling nervous too. The best way to get past nervousness is to own it and then face it. Again it's a very uncomfortable experience, and for some of us it can absolutely rule our lives. If nervousness is taking over in your life and you feel that it's controlling you, it might be a good idea to get some support from a counsellor. I took anti-depressant medication for a while. It helped a little bit to tone down my anxiety and this freed up some energy to help me explore ways of coping with my anxiety. The best thing that helped me was learning to accept myself and believe that I was a worthwhile person.

Alcohol

Many people enjoy alcohol and it can be lovely to share a glass of wine with good friends. Some people think that alcohol will help them to relax and allow them to interact better with others. I think this can be true, up to a point. If we drink too much alcohol it only depresses the nervous system and this means we will not perform at our best. Alcohol abuse will affect our judgement too and we might end up consenting to something we would usually not agree to. Some individuals believe 'to be a real man, you need to drink lots', but this is a fallacy. It takes more courage to say when you have had enough, than it does to just keep drinking. The important thing is that we take control of our alcohol intake and not allow it to take control of us.

Sex and sexuality

Sex and relationships are different things and one can have one without the other. They each add a different dimension to life and, some would argue, give a sense of adventure and intrigue that can be great fun and helpful in exploring aspects of life that are doubly interesting when shared with another.

How do we handle sexual desire?

Sexual desire is a feeling that most of us will experience. It is normal, healthy and, apart from helping to maintain the species, can lead to a loving and fulfilling experience. Sometimes this experience can be shared with another whom we willingly consent to have sex with. At other times the experience can be an individual one, one we choose to have with ourselves only. Masturbation is good news because usually one can find a private place (e.g. alone in one's own bedroom) where one can meet one's own sexual needs, so none of us has to be controlled by sexual desire when there isn't anyone else to share it with.

How old should I be for sex?

The age of consent for sex varies quite a lot from country to country and state to state within a country (for example in Great Britain the age of consent for heterosexual sex and homosexual sex is 16, but in Northern Ireland it is 17 for homosexuality; in Western Australia the age of consent for heterosexual sex is 16, but for homosexual sex it is 21).

Many 17-year-olds are still virgins and this is OK. Losing one's virginity is not connected to how old you are but to when you feel ready and comfortable to share in sexual intercourse with another person. Some would say that it takes courage to say 'no' to sexual intercourse and to choose to wait until you believe you are ready.

Sex with children is never allowed and is not legal. This is because children are not physically or emotionally ready for sex, their bodies are too immature and sex could damage them. It's also because sex is an adult encounter for individuals who understand what it means. It's not always easy to determine the age of another individual, so how do we know if they are too young or not? At times being with individuals who enjoy the same things that we do and whom we can relate to might mean relating to people much younger than us. Having fun and time together is fine, but they might not be the right candidates for a sexual relationship. It's important to establish these facts and to know how old someone is. A good way to be discreet about this is to talk about birthdays and ask when their birthday is. You can say how old you will be at your next birthday and you can ask them how old they will be, what they might do for their birthday and what gifts they hope for. Even though we might be sexually attracted to someone we have fun with, we must not have sex with them if they are under the age of consent, even if they appear to be happy to have a sexual relationship.

Do I have to involve other people in my sexuality, or can I handle it myself?

Sex with oneself can be fulfilling and satisfying, even though it does not involve anyone else. Sex with another can teach us about another person's experience and take us beyond ourselves. A relationship implies that there are two of you and this is where it can get interesting! Most of us like the idea of relating to someone else. Most of us have some experience of relationships and this isn't always a good experience. The good news, though, is that each relationship is different and they don't have to present us with the same problems each time. Whilst it's true that we take all of our 'past baggage' from previous relationships into our next one, we can also take all of our learning and gleaned understanding too. Statistically, one in two first marriages breaks down, so even the most socially equipped amongst us human beings are not guaranteed success in this area. So how do we measure success? Maybe staying married for a season is a success story, even if it didn't last a lifetime?

Is it OK to say 'no' to sex? Will it mean we can still be friends?

Yes, it is OK to say 'no' to sex. Sometimes some people will only want sex and will not be interested in being friends. If this is the case then they would not make good friends for us anyway, so it's best to move on to relating to others who are more likely to want to know us for who we are and not just what they can get from us.

How will I know when the occasion or moment is right to talk
about relationships and sexuality?

I don't know that there is a right 'moment'. I usually talk about things
and see where the conversation leads me. I also check in often with
my friend and give them a chance to tell me if they are comfortable
with talking about a particular subject or not, and if it's the right time
and place for them.

CHAPTER 4

Being in a Partnership

When we have sorted out the facts and ideas about relationship in general; thought about whether or not we would like to relate romantically to another person or not; and then considered how to go about it all; we are in a position to go further. For most of us heterosexuality will be the term that defines how we feel. This means that our sexual orientation and preference will be for the opposite sex. During our discovery of 'self', though, it's not unusual to go through a stage of either feeling sexually attracted to the same sex or at least wanting to discover what a sexual encounter with someone of the same sex would be like. For many people this exploration, often occurring during adolescence, is a one-off experience and doesn't lead them into any long-term desire for the same sex. For those of us who do discover our sexual orientation is not heterosexual, although we will be in the minority, it is important to know that our experience is valid and important.

There are many demands and implications associated with being heterosexual. For instance, if you are a single adult there is an expectation that you won't be happy on your own. It is an accepted norm amongst the NT population that to be happy one needs to know the joy of partnering another in a romantic relationship. Of course, even though one knows this is not necessarily the case, it is still a belief that places unnecessary demands and expectations upon many individuals. One of the questions I am asked by parents is: 'Will he/she be able to have a relationship? Will they marry and have a family?' I understand the anxiety behind these questions; parents want the best life possible for their offspring. For the parents, being 'in a relationship' and sharing their life with another is seen as the route to fulfilment and completion. The normal role for adults is to work, marry, have kids and pass on the family name with all its tradition and heritage. It's quite difficult for many parents to imagine that their off-spring might be 'happy' even if they don't have a partner to share their life with. In reality, of course, many NT individuals are happy with their single life and choose career above family life. The other part of this reality, though, is that usually individuals who choose such a vocation have close friends and/or family and they do not live as islands.

So, maybe, if we are parents of a child with ASD, the question we should be asking is: 'Will s/he be able to form friendships and live interdependently?' The answer will vary according to how develop-mentally delayed an individual with ASD might be, whether they un-derstand the concept and whether or not they recognize the need for other people in their lives. If the question we are asking relates to our-selves, as adults, then it really is 'Do we want to have a romantic at-traction with another individual?' If our answer is 'yes' or if we are already in such a relationship but are unsure of how to continue so as to maximize our chances of success, then we are in a good position to find answers to our questions. If we think we know it all or we fail to recognize our role and responsibility in any given relationship, then we should not expect our relationships to grow and develop in a healthy way.

Demands and expectations

How do I explore my needs and those of my partner?

For those of us who choose to be in a relationship and partnership long-term and are fortunate enough to find a partner who wants the same thing, life will present another set of demands and expectations.

It seems likely that the expectations our parents placed upon us (that we would want a partner; that once we had a partner we would want to understand them; that we would be interested in the 'world' our partner occupies; that we will want the same things as our partner and dream the same dreams, and so on) will now become the expecta-tions and demands of our relationship. Those expectations, however, will differ from person to person and be influenced by whether one is polytropic or monotropic, and by whether one is partnered by some-one who is polytropic or monotropic or a unique combination of both. For example, if both of you are on the autistic spectrum, you will both have a monotropic disposition.

This is true of my partner and me and has resulted in a variety of conflicts that we are usually able to sort out because we understand our monotropism. If, however, we did not have the understanding that we do, our relationship would be one of constant misunderstand-ing and confusion. It has taken us years to reach the point in our relat-ing to one another that we enjoy today. Those years have been quite tumultuous at times; each of us believed the discord and insult experi-ences we were having were being purposely caused by the other. Once we recognized the reality that our experiences were a result of non-understanding of each other and we worked to change that, things between us changed to a more positive outcome.

Listening to another person talk about who they are, what they like and want from us is a vital aspect in any relationship. The diffi-culty for us though is that we might not find this interesting. Even though we are interested in the person themselves, listening to them talk might be uninteresting. We still need to listen though. When I first encountered this I felt really uncomfortable in these situations, I wasn't interested and couldn't see the point of the conversation. Now I know that the point is 'this person needs to talk and express these things to me'. They feel comfortable and confident with me: enough to share who they are, what they like, and so on. They need to do this, and I am honoured that they feel safe enough to do this with me. I don't have to 'feel' interested, but I do have to 'show' interest. I do this by listening to them and by giving them my support.

My Love

It wasn't always this way. The joy of knowing you
And sharing in your life has taught me that I am
Able to love and accept myself. In your presence
I come to life in a way that I have never experienced before.
This rag doll who is losing her stuffing becomes the musical clown,
So full of colour and vitality.

You set me free from the demands of self-introspection
And its ugly forest of gloom.
In its place I am able to walk through sunlit woods
And enjoy choruses of bird song.

Your smile delights my eyes and the peace in my soul
Rolls over me like the gentle waves of a calm ocean.
So soothing is your voice to my ears that even the roar
Of my lions within cannot shatter it.
Thank you, my love, for your quiet assurance and humble
vulnerability.
To you I owe a never-ending debt, my life.

Being 'in love'

Love certainly can be a 'loopy state' as my friend Dinah Murray put it.
It's a rather wonderful state, though, and one that can seem to open
doors of emotion not experienced before. Of course this can be scary,
traumatic, invigorating, all-consuming and incredibly restorative, all
at the same time. 'Love makes the world go round', they say. 'Love
makes one's heart sing and puts a spring in our step', they say. These
expressions lead one to believe that love is a wonderful thing and
without it life is incomplete. In many ways this is true and each of us is
designed to be loved and to give love. My only concern with the
'romanticizing' of love is that it doesn't prepare us for the harsh
realities of partnership. We need to enjoy the warm and safe emotions
associated with being loved and with loving another, but we also
need to be prepared to expect rough and bumpy roads that come with
love. When sharing our lives with another person in the intimacy of a
loving relationship we are required to build good foundations of
loyalty, trust, commitment, honesty, courage and even vulnerability.
These will help us ride out the storm when the feelings of 'love'
waver. I like the words of a song I know by Don Fransisco: 'Love is
not a feeling it's an act of your will'. These words have helped me
through many a 'rough' patch in my relationships.

Real expectations

Expectation and demand can be healthy or they can be misplaced, selfish and overbearing. For example, I expect mutual respect and acceptance of who we are as people and as individuals in my relationships, but I do not expect to be the only person of importance or value in those relationships. I cannot and indeed should not be the only person to meet all the needs of my partner. Our partners have their own lives, autonomy and multiple needs that require the input of different individuals at different times for different reasons. I am just one individual with my individual contribution and, although that is unique, special and specific, it will not meet all the needs of another individual.

Will our needs be different?

Are the needs of neuro-typicals different to our needs? For example, the need for confirmation and reassurance in a relationship: do they need this? Yes they do, is the short answer. The thing to remember, though, is that we are all different and some of us need more reassurance than others. I know that if my partner and I (we are both on the autistic spectrum, we are both monotropic) have a disagreement and we are left with feelings of misunderstanding, rejection and sadness, then we both interpret this literally and, temporarily, will believe that we are not loved by the other any more. Such reactions are intense, dramatic and will override all of our previous experience, so much so that we can both move into a place of being completely sure that the other will leave us! So, I constantly need to check that my partner still wants me and still loves me. This may seem irritating and frustrating, but we both have talked about our need for reassurance and we both accept that this is how it is for us. I know other ASD couples who appear to be the opposite. Their sense of individual autonomy is strong and they seem to need little ongoing reassurance of their commitment and love for one another.

What about needs for shared and individual time, affection, hobbies, sexual intimacy and time relating to non-couple activities? These needs will differ for couples and individuals, so it's a good idea to check in with your partner and talk about the needs you both have.

For example, my partner and I love to go for walks in the countryside. But my walking pace is much slower. So, we walk together sometimes and at other times my partner needs to be able to enjoy a walk without me. I know some women who love to go shopping, but they only enjoy this when they go alone or with another person who can enjoy shopping too. There are many individuals who don't like to go shopping, and so they do something else whilst their partner shops with someone else. It doesn't mean that because the two of you don't always have the same interest you are not interested in each other. It just means that you are different people who bring difference into your relationship and such differences need to be accommodated.

Sexual intimacy

When it comes to sexual intimacy some of us have different ideas about our own needs and the needs of others. Some people like lots of touch, kissing and foreplay; the actual act of intercourse seems secondary to the time of sharing in mutual physical affection. Other people find too much touch overloading; this can actually close down their sexual pleasure so much that they cannot continue with sexual activity. If one partner likes it one way and the other partner likes it the other way there will be conflict. Addressing such conflict and talking about it can be helpful. Exploring ways of meeting the needs of both parties is essential if the relationship is to continue. I have known of couples who need to wear gloves to reduce the overload of direct contact. Others spend time with candlelight in a foaming bath where the effects of direct touch can be minimized but the time of intimacy can be maximized.

THE LEGACY OF SEXUAL ABUSE

The section below might be anyone's experience. If you have been sexually abused or wronged you too might identify with the description below. Sexual abuse is all too common and, unfortunately, is not always taken seriously by our communities. However, it will leave us vulnerable to all kinds of emotions: anger, fear, frustration, and even no feelings at all. As a child I was sexually abused. For many years, although I experienced a healthy sex drive I seemed incapable of sexual fulfilment. Although the story below is not mine, it could have been.

Ever since I can remember I have had a very strong desire for sex. As a small child I masturbated indiscriminately and seemed unaware of others. As I grew older I became a sex object for boys and men who took advantage of my inability to understand what were 'grown-up' games and what was inappropriate for children. I was sexually abused from the age of 4 until I was 13 years old.

At he age of 14 I had a 'steady' boyfriend. This boy was quite handsome and he seemed to like to kiss and fondle me. I wasn't really into him but I liked the way he made me feel. My difficulty in our relationship though was that I got bored really quickly and couldn't really relax with him. I also became quickly overloaded with too much sensory stimulation.

Maybe part of the reason I didn't like intimacy with him was the molestation I had gone through as a child, but I think in retrospect it was more about sensory issues. Some touch I liked and some I didn't. His body pressing up against mine was difficult for me to handle at times. It didn't feel like I thought it would.

At times I enjoyed some of the things he did, but overall the experience was unpleasant to me. This was a scenario that repeated itself with other boyfriends I had. I never really felt 'at home' or comfortable in sexual activity. My raging hormones would drive me to try sex and each time I hoped it would be different, but it just didn't work out that way, and I was constantly disappointed.

I loved to watch the feature programs on the television where couples seemed so fulfilled by one another but, for me, my frustration only increased and I just couldn't locate satisfaction. My hormones and body kept telling me that I wanted to enjoy sexual intimacy, but the actual experience left me feeling grubby and even angry.

Today I understand that part of my difficulties were due to the sexual abuse I went through as a child. When I finally found a loving patient partner who was happy to take time with me and go slowly things began to improve.

Over the years it has become easier to relate sexually and without anger. However, I still have moments when I do not want to be touched, or touched a certain way. I am fortunate to have a partner who loves and accepts me for who I am.

Sexual abuse may predispose us to all sorts of difficulties with sexual intimacy. Some individuals may feel driven obsessively to being sexually active with lots of strangers they don't really know. It's as if our bodies crave intimacy but our emotions and minds don't quite know how to correlate this successfully. Our previous experiences might have left us feeling 'wanting', wounded and with a belief system that we are only good if we allow someone else to 'use' us. The other belief might be that rather than be controlled by others we need to be 'in control', so we aim to 'use' them instead. Neither of these beliefs are helpful, even though they are understandable. If we want to stop being victimized we need to take back our control and that of others and change it to learning how to be 'in tune' with ourselves and with others. Slowing the pace down might help us to gain time so we can decide what the appropriate behaviour might be and not rush into something we might regret later.

SENSORY ISSUES

Sensory issues are much more common for us than they seem to be for NT individuals. There are things we can do to address these though. The first thing is to recognize the problem then we can explore what to do about it. We can spend some time attempting to raise our thresholds for touch. For example, we can draw soft material across our body so as to help desensitize it. Using a soft brush, three to six times in one direction, three times a day on our arms and legs may help us to get used to touch. We may like firm touch but not cope with touch if it isn't firm. Telling our partner that we need this is good, it lets them know we are not rejecting them, we just need their 'touch' to be firm.

Sometimes a specific tone of voice can be painful to us. If we intend to continue to build a relationship with someone whose voice hurts our ears, letting them know that we need to turn our head in order to listen to them, or that we need them to lower their voice, is important. If we just walk away, raise the level of our own talking or turn up the television, they might think we are not interested in them.

Sometimes our partner might like to use a specific aftershave or perfume that really 'gets up our nose' and we can't cope with the fragrance. The smell seems to cling to us and we can't get away from it. We need to let them know that this is happening so that they can change the fragrance and either use one that is more tolerable or not wear one at all.

Some individuals don't feel 'dressed' without jewellery. However, their joy might cause another great discomfort. The noise from the jewellery, the distraction or the way it hangs or sits upon a person might cause discomfort and even fear for another person.

Sometimes specific colour, material, texture and even shape can negatively impact upon us and we may feel scared, physically unwell, tormented or irritated by these things. These are all things we can do something about if we explain them to our partner and they are sympathetic to our plight.

Learning how to express our concerns in a safe environment takes time, and unfortunately many NT individuals take things personally and tend to feel rejected or unwanted. Explaining that you want *them* but don't want the discomfort of sensory overload *they bring with them* is crucial.

HOW MUCH TALKING SHOULD I DO?

There isn't a rule about how much talking is enough. Again, I check this out with my partner and allow their response to me to guide my talking. I have a tendency to talk too much in general anyway, so I give my partner (who talks much less than me) the 'right' to tell me if I've talked too much and need to be quiet for a while.

CAN I ACCEPT MYSELF IF I HAVE UNUSUAL TURN-ONS?

Being turned on sexually could be described as a biological wonder! By this I mean that we often don't have much of a say in what turns us on. Different things are a turn-on for different people. One man's poison is another's pleasure! So, yes, we can accept ourselves if we have unusual 'turn-ons'. The rule is that as long as I respect myself and other people, I'm probably doing OK. I know of some people who are turned on by mystery and intrigue, others by pornography, and some by large noses! Remember sex with children under the age of consent is never OK.

Reality sets in

Come as you are

Although when we are dating and discovering about love and romance we might 'dress up' for the occasion and try really hard to present only our 'good' side to the person we are building a relationship with, this cannot be maintained. There will come a time when we just can't keep up the performance. Seeing one another 'at our worst' is one of the true tests of whether a relationship is sound and strong or whether it is built upon a flimsy foundation of things that won't survive the daily demands of real life. For example, if we are only attracted to someone because of their good looks and sexual appeal, we will be in for a rude awakening as we age, experience times of ill health, and the times when libido sleeps! We need also to love and accept the person as they are, beyond the physical. What of their personality? Do you like the person they are? What of their values and dreams – do you share them? What of their grievances and pain – can you respect them? The bottom line is 'Can you see yourself waking up with this person beside you in 50 years' time?' If the answer is 'yes', all well and good. If you are unsure, you might need to check out your motives for relating to this person.

The everyday nitty-gritty of relating

Once when I was really worried about the 'not feeling much' in my relationship, I talked to a friend who told me that if we were always feeling in great intensity, we would be tired and worn out very quickly. She said that it was very normal and quite usual to have times when one's feelings are very intense and times when they are not. She told me that it didn't mean the love I had once 'felt' had gone away, just that it was settling in and becoming very much part of my everyday life. It was such a relief to hear this and to know that all was well. When my partner came home at the end of the day and smiled at me, I knew it was as my friend had suggested. Although I didn't feel great waves of emotion, I did feel comfy and at home. This state of being with my partner is the one that I have come to treasure, and I now realize that this is what it means to 'come home'.

There are times when relating to another person is very trying indeed. Each person we relate to has their own set of life demands, and it might mean that they are not always available to us in the way that we would want. I'm still learning that my demands can just be too much at times for others to handle and I need to give them space from me just like I need space away from them. I tell myself at such times that, although I feel a bit uncomfortable when this happens, discomfort does not amount to 'I'm not wanted any more', it's just a temporary feeling and it will go away.

I have been known to experience feelings of complete abandonment, and separation anxiety sets in very quickly. This can happen when 'the beloved' has not been in contact for a whole day! At times it feels like when the person is present we have a relationship but when they go away then the relationship goes too. Actually my feelings are wrong. My relationship continues even though the person may be hidden from view. What I find helpful at these times is to have a photograph, movie clip or words, which have been given to me, that I can attend to as often as I like, and then I am reminded that my relationship is intact even if they are away.

I'm a person too

At times being in a relationship might lead to our own sense of 'self' feeling rather submerged in all the daily demands of life. At first, when love is young and one doesn't have a mortgage, there is more time, money and energy to devote to being romantic. After time and perhaps children, the financial and emotional demands upon one's time become a little overstretched. This can leave one feeling tired, depressed and a bit lost beneath it all. Please, if this is how you are feeling don't give up. What you most likely need is to find a way to recreate some 'time' just for you.

Time alone

I can remember feeling guilty because I stayed longer than I needed to in the bathroom. Here, in the smallest room in the house, I could escape demand. It's OK to need time for self and time to rediscover the 'you' under all that weight of responsibility. The children do grow up! There comes a time when their need of your intervention will be reduced. This is good. In the meantime though, give yourself a break. Maybe a weekend away once a month would suit you. Maybe you have other family members you could ask to baby sit or house sit for you. Perhaps you could join a club or take up an activity that interests you. One of the best things I did was taking myself back to school. After completing the high-school certificate at the age of 40 I went on to university, which brought new adventure into my life. Studying hard and achieving good results did great things for my self-esteem too!

If we don't take good care of ourselves, as well as of our relationships with others, we will be in danger of our own personhood being eaten away by demand. In the long run we could be quite resentful of missed opportunities, which will negatively impact upon us and upon those around us.

Changing relationships

All relationships change over time and, if we are busy with our own affairs, we might not notice the changes. Some change is welcome and healthy. Some change might not be so good. How can we tell the difference? I think that the indicators of 'wholesome' change have distinctive markings. For example, any 'change' in our relationships that brings us closer together and makes us feel ultimately more comfortable, that helps us understand ourselves and our partners better, is good. Any change that increases the gulf between us, makes us feel unwelcome and serves only to alienate us from our partner is bad. Having said this, however, we do need to check that our perception, which is feeding our emotions, is correct. I know at times I feel unwelcome when my partner needs time and space to avoid overload, but actually it's not me that is unwelcome, it's the demand I bring with me. Learning how to separate these issues and talk about them together is vital to the health of any relationship.

Dying relationships

Death is a natural part of life, but it doesn't make it any easier to come to terms with. When my first partner and I could no longer relate as a married couple I felt an enormous feeling of guilt. I had taken my marriage vows with utter sincerity and believed that marriage was forever, 'until death do us part'. The reality was that neither I nor my husband was happy in our relationship. We were different people going in different directions, and even though we tried to align ourselves with mutuality, it didn't work. Slowly but surely our relationship died. I went to see a counsellor, and after some time in counselling she told me that I needed 'a respectable divorce'. She explained that my relationship was dead and that I was carrying a corpse around upon my shoulders. The weight of this death was too much and I needed release from it. 'So, this is what "until death do us part" might mean', I thought. It was quite a revelation and one that I shall be eternally grateful for.

Separation is a difficult experience to travel though. Just like it takes time to adjust to being in a partnership, it takes time to adjust to being single again. The feeling of my being a 'bad wife' and the disappointment of failure hung around me like a bad smell. I thought it would never go away! But, as time went on and new opportunities opened up for me, fresh air came into my life, along with new relationships and a sense of my life being worthwhile. Revived autonomy and self-value are essential ingredients to recovery from separation. They are not automatically generated, though; they require our attention and interaction. We need to take back the control and get moving again. A friend once told me that a car with the engine running won't go anywhere until it's in gear and is empowered by a bit of throttle!

Divorce

I have heard of individuals celebrating divorce as a means to an end. That is, celebrating that finality of separation is a rite of passage that formalizes the parting of the ways for two people who, at one stage in their lives, were walking along the same path. I have passed through divorce and come out the other side, alive! It wasn't a pleasant experience, and it isn't one I would wish to repeat. The important thing to remember is that none of us goes into a relationship expecting it to end. We all make our commitments to marriage and our partners with the hope that a lifetime of love and harmony awaits us. The problem is that marriage is made for fallible human beings whose lives and circumstances change. Sometimes we can accommodate the changes we face and sometimes we cannot.

It might be difficult to think of divorce as 'right' but I do believe that there are times when it is wrong to stay married so divorce is the only other response. Divorce is also a respectable funeral that buries the death of a relationship. If we don't bury our dead, then we carry with us the aroma of decaying material that gives off a stench that affects all those around us. One of the difficult things, though, is deciding when the moment of death has occurred and how to go about dealing with it.

If you are in a situation that has a smell of decay about it maybe you need to talk to friends, family or a trained relationship counsellor and take some advice. No one wants to bury something if there are still signs of life, so you might need to explore the possibilities.

Single parenting

Being a single parent does not have to mean that our kids miss out. Did you know that in the bird and animal world many offspring are reared by one parent? Take squirrels, for example: reared by their maternal parent only, they seem none the worse for it. In the wild the female squirrel is pursued by many male suitors; after an exhausting hike between the trees and their branches, the female allows herself to be mated by the most robust male. She then goes off to her drey, gives birth and stays with her young until time for them to leave. With sea-horses it is the male who carries the eggs, hatches and nurses the young. It seems odd to me that, even though we know of the variety of parenting options amongst our animal friends, we still claim that human children need two parents of opposite gender to 'turn out OK'. I want to say how illogical this is. In fact, it seems to me that the belief that a child needs two parents to be 'balanced' is more myth than reality. How many individuals do you know whose parents were shining examples of 'togetherness' and whose commitment to each other outshone every dark moment of their lives? I know a few, but I don't know many. Even those families where there are two genetic parents, quite often it is only one of the parents that is involved with practical parenting.

In an ideal world parenting of human offspring should be the job of two parents. It's just great when both parents are involved with their offspring in their practical, emotional and supportive adventures. But when this is not a possibility, one would hope that society at large would not pass judgement, rather it would see fit to support its fellow human beings in any and every way possible. What could be more important than bringing up the next generation? Whether or not a child has two attentive parents should not be the most important question. What we should be asking is 'Does this family have the support and resources it needs to thrive?' There are plenty of families with two parents who may not be equipped to bring up their child. Families need support, whatever type of family unit they are formed from.

Wendy, aged 4, with her younger sister Alison and Rusty, their Aunty Bett and Uncle Charlie's dog.

Wendy as a mature student. From a 'no-hoper' at school to a university graduate!

Wendy and Beatrice, 1996

Wendy, Beatrice and the children when they were young, 1984
Timmy, on Wendy's knee, aged 2, Katy, aged 8, Matthew, aged 4 and Guy, aged 10.

Katy, Wendy's daughter, getting married to Stuart in 2004
Family picture with Beatrice, Katy, Stuart and Wendy in front row. Wendy's sister-in-law,
Margaret, sister, cousin Julie, Cameron (nephew's son) and niece, Vanessa in middle row.
Brother, Tony, nephew Jason, Vanessa's hubby Kevin and nephew Alistair in back row.

Katy, her brother Tim and Wendy at Katy's wedding, 2004

Matthew, aged 19, only weeks before his death in 1999

Beatrice, Wendy, her oldest son Guy, his girlfriend Anna and Tye the dog, 2003

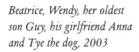

CHAPTER 5

Discovering Bisexuality, Homosexuality or Transgender Dispositions

What does it mean to grow up with ASD and be bisexual, homosexual or transsexual? Does this mean a lot of stress? Are there some advantages to being 'bi', gay or transsexual and autistic? How easy is it to own our sexuality?

Gender identity

As individuals, we are growing and developing in a number of ways. We each have our own personality, characteristics, gender and sexual orientation. Being born with a particular physical gender identity does not automatically predispose us towards wanting to relate romantically and sexually to the opposite sex. We may experience times of attraction to the same sex and to the opposite sex. We may experience attraction only to someone of the same sex as ourselves.

At times, for some of us, we may feel more at home in pursuits, activities and clothing that are usually associated with the opposite sex to our own. For example, as a woman I prefer wearing men's clothing. Clothing designed for men is usually stronger, better made, less expensive and fits me better than clothing designed for women. Modern Western society does not frown upon my chosen attire. However, if I were a male who preferred commonly attributed female pursuits (wearing make-up and carrying a handbag) and dressed in female attire (skirts, frocks and high-heel shoes), I would not be afforded the same acceptance.

Why do we have these different standards? Why is it more acceptable in Western society to be female and act and dress like a male than it is to be male and act and dress like a female? Well, unfortunately I think it comes down to what we feel most threatened by. I believe society sees the male as being desirable and strong, even in a woman. The female is seen as 'the weaker sex' and when males take a female form upon themselves, this is seen as lowering themselves in some way. It is very threatening to the traditional Western lifestyle. There are exceptions of course! If a male is a dancer, hairdresser or in the theatre and has 'female' attributes, these may be seen as more acceptable and even welcomed!

Homosexuality and ASD

Recently I read an article in the British Medical Journal. The following is a quote from that article.

> The survival value of homosexuality for the human species is to be found in its effect on population growth. Anyone who is worried about environmental degradation caused by the growth of the human population should promote homosexuality. Indeed, it would be desirable if most people became homosexual and only a small, selected proportion of humans of every recognizable subgroup attended to the modest reproductive needs of the species.
>
> All the effort, emotion, and money spent on family planning could be saved, and disgusting and unnatural practices of contraception – such as genital mutilation, various prophylactic methods, and even withdrawal and the observance of cervical mucus – could be done away with. Indeed, homosexual sex is akin to organic farming inasmuch as it eschews artifice, yet it yields pleasure and elation and, often, pure love.
>
> The ideal social organization of mankind in this overcrowded world would be one in which the majority lived in homosexual monogamy. If homosexuality became the norm, population numbers would decline precipitously. (Loefler 2004, p.1325)

OK this might seem a bit over the top, but I hope you can see the point here. Most of the arguments that ridicule and present homosexuality as unnatural, degrading and immoral fall apart when one considers the wider thoughts as expressed above. Having an orientation that is not heterosexual but homosexual is just as moral and as important as being heterosexual. I believe that it too is part of nature's design and overall plan to protect and enhance the diversity of the human species.

Being a person on the autistic spectrum, being monotropic, will mean we are part of a minority group. Being autistic and homosexual will marginalize us even more. Does this have to be a problem? No it does not, but it might present us with extra difficulties that require some navigation. For example, if you are female, autistic and homosexual, your opportunities of finding a partner to share your life with might be reduced more than if you were male, autistic and homosexual. I'm saying this because statistically there seem to be more males in both the world of ASD and in the world of homosexuality.

In Chapter 9 you can read more about my personal experience of ASD and homosexuality – what it meant for me and my family, and my decision to live in an openly 'gay' relationship. However, it's important to understand that we are all different, and this will also be true of our experiences; even if we have the same labels on our diagnosis and gender orientation, our life journeys can be different. I am sharing mine with you in the hope that it might be helpful. Accepting my ASD and my homosexuality are two decisions I am happy that I made.

Being 'bi'

Although some statistics suggest that up to 10 per cent of the population is homosexual I think the statistics for bisexuality will be higher. There are many individuals within our communities who are attracted to both sexes but who choose to partner or marry a person of the opposite sex. For them, life can be very satisfying, up to a point. I know women who are married who dearly love and care for their husbands, but who miss the closeness associated with a lesbian relationship. For some individuals acceptance of their bisexuality means they have come to terms with their sexual needs and confine them to their fantasies, whilst for others fantasy isn't enough and they have other lovers.

'Being bisexual doubles your chances of a date on a Saturday night' (Woody Allen). Although this quote might make us smile, I don't think dating is that easy for most of us. Being bi and autistic might present an individual with lots of confusion and emotional pain. What is one to do when one feels such strong attraction to either sex? Does it mean that the individual doesn't fit into any camp but straddles the fence across both? Or does it mean that there is a third 'gender camp' where being 'bi' is a unique identity too? I guess that the whole topic of sexuality is more complex than most of us realize! I reckon whatever our sexual orientation is, it's what we do with it that counts. Again, respecting ourselves and others is the key. We are human beings with a variety of needs and desires. Some of those needs and desires we can fulfil, and others we might not be able to. Feelings are one thing and actions are another. If we spend our lives in promiscuity hoping to somehow complete who we are, we might be disappointed. If we start off feeling good about who we are, though, and being in a place where we understand and accept ourselves, the story will be different. In fact, we won't be looking to others to fill us up, we will be exploring what it is that we can give back to the world we are all part of.

Doubly Drawn

Your smile and eyes come dance with mine,
Your arms around me tight.
I love your voice, your youth, your prime,
Our laughter as we fight.

Your maleness and your softness,
Attract the woman in me,
Your long piano fingers,
That promise to set love free.

As much as I so love your form,
I miss the female charm.

At times I long for tender touch,
The womanly kiss, I miss so much.

What am I to do with all these things I feel?
They take over my life and present as so real.
But this reality may not have a place,
I'm torn in two by each different face.

This world with all its rules and taboos,
Does not allow for love that duals,
That switches off from thee to me,
From she to he and back to me!

I'm somewhere in between the two,
My love for him and love for you.
In an ideal world you both would do,
But I know my ideal cannot come true.

So, as a way of compromise,
And to avoid regret,
Longing for the both of you
I live my life, a secret.

Acceptance by others?
Could be a dream come true.
Oh to be just understood,
You'll see I'm just like you.

Whatever our sexual orientation is and whatever we feel about who we are, we will be influenced by our belief systems. Being different because we are individuals on the ASD spectrum takes time to adjust to. Being different from the majority because of our sexual orientation will also take us time to get used to. For a very long time I battled with my sexual orientation. I prayed and prayed that it would go away. I felt betrayed and angry that I was designed to feel attraction only to someone of the same sex. I think most of my discomfort was based upon false beliefs that being different was bad.

Being different isn't bad, it's just different. Yes, there are some disadvantages to being autistic and gay. We will find it difficult to locate other individuals who will accept us for ourselves. Most of my friends tried to change me. Even my family tried to make both my ASD and my homosexuality go away. The best thing that I did was stop believing that I was bad and recognize that other people are uncomfortable around us because they don't understand us. I keep company as much as possible with others who accept and encourage me to be myself. We can't change the world in one hit but we can stop the world changing us. Bit by bit, as others come to know us they too might find that we are human beings with legitimate needs. In the meantime we need to look after ourselves and foster a belief system that supports who we are and does not attack us.

Is our life course set?

Although we each are the product of nature and nurture, it's not only our genes or the influence of others that make us who we are. We are also the product of our own decisions. I choose what and how much I eat; no one forces that choice upon me. I choose how much exercise I will or will not get each day. I choose what I watch on the television, and so on. We can also choose who we listen to, what those words do for us and what we think about things. At times it might seem like we don't have a choice, especially if we are not able to move away from the negative influences on our lives. However, I reckon we can take control over our lives. When I am not wanting to subject myself to the negativity of others, I can listen to my walkman; turn over the television channel or turn it off; state that I am not happy with the conversation and request the person to refrain from speaking in such a way; take myself out for a walk; read a book or phone a friend, and so on.

I do not have to listen to negative words being spoken over or about me, nor do you. We can set our own course if we allow ourselves to explore positive ways to do this. For example, I chose to return to study. Some of my friends decided to travel abroad and visit other countries. Some of my other friends joined a local singing club in their village. Whatever you decide, do it for you and because it gives you life and meaning. Allowing other people to dictate who we are will only cause us to resent them, and we might even end up angry with ourselves for allowing it all to happen. We might not be able to change our sexual orientation but this is only one aspect of our lives, it does not have to completely rule the rest of our lives.

The courage to be yourself

Being brave is not the thing that I do best. When I am physically unwell or if I hurt myself somehow, I can get very upset very easily. This is also true for me if I experience my friends being upset with me. Maybe you know what I mean? At times I really wanted to go somewhere or do something but the friend I was with had other ideas. So I would let go of what I wanted to do and accommodate them. Over time, however, I began to question the things that were happening for me. One of those was that I didn't really express my needs or desires and this was causing a disquiet within me. So I started to say to my friends the things that I thought about, dreamt about, wanted or wished for.

It does take courage to share with those closest to you in an intimate way. Talking about our dream partner, our same-sex desires or our longing to be set free from a gender that doesn't fit us, is not an easy thing to do. For many years I lived with the desire for a sex change. I didn't 'feel' feminine, and most of the female roles expected of me I was uncomfortable with. As a child, I loved to climb trees, go fishing, keep lizards and snakes, collect insects and keep rodents. As a teenager, I loved to be around piston engines (especially the older English motor bikes), construct things out of wood, play soccer and hang out with the lads. As a young adult, I shared some of my pursuits with a young man and we eventually married. Although I loved decorating my home and painting murals on the walls, I didn't relish the role of 'housewife'. Eventually my children were born and I loved being a Mum… But, inside my body I still didn't feel like a woman, whatever that is meant to be.

When I was young I was pretty well flat-chested. I easily passed as a male youth. Whenever someone called me 'son' I felt pleased and at home. To help me feel more comfortable in my female body I tried to 'become' more feminine. I had my ears pierced, grew my hair long and wore long dresses. But it didn't make a difference. I could dress up as much as I liked, I still didn't feel female. In my forties I had the tops of my arms tattooed. On my left arm I had a rainbow with stars and a pathway depicting the journey of life. On my right arm I had an oak leaf tattooed with acorns on a branch and a butterfly. These tattoos symbolized strength (an acorn will push its way through concrete) courage (butterflies are deaf) and the way ahead opening up for me (stars and a pathway, always there above the clouds) plus, of course, the rainbow – a symbol that my life would not become overwhelmed and flooded by too much 'stuff' ever again. I began to accept that, yes, I am female, but, yes, I feel more male than female. For some of us this is how it is. For whatever reason, as a woman I am more masculine than some and, the good news is, this is OK!

Accepting how we feel isn't always easy and, for some, feeling trapped in a body that yells the opposite to what we feel, and what is expected of us, and so on, can be just too difficult. I have known young people commit suicide rather than live their lives with the confusion and pain of transgender issues. Before you judge us, try to see things from our perspective. If you cannot, then at least accept that we exist and we need your support. It is so much easier to cope with our load when we feel understood. Just because we are individuals on the autistic spectrum, we are not immune from transgender issues. If anything, because we are monotropic, we may well be completely consumed by our transgender feelings and quite obsessive about our cross-gender identity. If this is the case, what might be helpful is either finding a community where we are accepted (e.g. a place or field of employment) or being able to live in the world as the gender identity we feel most at home in (e.g. living as a woman although we have a male body, or living as a male even though we have a female body).

Drawing and dreaming

Sometimes, as individuals with ASD, we can be emotionally attached to objects. As Pukki (2003) noted, 'the tendency to relate sexually to unusual aspects of the environment or people seems to be very much ignored' (p.60). She goes on to say that 'part of what is actually expression of sexuality might go unnoticed as "ritual and routine" type activity' (p.60).

Drawing of 'breasts like mountains'

Before I could live openly in a gay relationship I lived obsessively within a fantasy world that was governed by the female form. I painted murals on brick garage walls of circles within circles. I drew, dreamed and wrote poetry about all and everything that was soft, female and breast-like. I would curl up against firm surfaces and suck the roof of my mouth. I didn't do these things in public but this is where I lived. I have always loved circular objects, especially if they were smooth and squashy. It was not until I was in my thirties that my obsession with circles began to make sense to me and I finally understood its underlying message. Finding a partner who accepts my egocentricities and even welcomes who I am has been a miracle. When this happens to a person it is just wondrous. I value the scripture 'You shall know the truth and the truth shall set you free'.

Garage wall 'breasts'

Now, within a committed relationship where I am free to experience appropriate sexual expression I am no longer driven to draw circles!

For each of us, finding the truth of who we are and being free to live that truth is liberating. Being an individual with ASD and being different because of sexual orientation too, is much more common than we think. I know several individuals with ASD who are gay, bi or transsexual. Just like you, we each need a place to call home.

Fabric 'breasts' on wall

Table 5.1 aims to illustrate typical adolescent development and development for adolescents with ASD/Asperger's syndrome. Although it is obvious that physical development is similar and there are stages we all recognize, one's gender identity is not so obvious. If we appreciate that gender identity is formed in the brain, probably in utero, then we should also understand that this is not something we can have a choice about. The stage of rapid brain growth that we go through during puberty will accelerate gender identity issues.

So, what next?

Learning to accept and love myself just the way I am is one thing, but what do I do after that? Not all of us will succeed in finding a partner to share our lives with. Some of us are not interested in a long-term relationship. We might discover that we are happy in our work, careers, with our families, pets and friendships, without a 'special' person or partnership. This is good. The main thing to consider here is that we are happy with our lot.

Table 5.1 Adolescence – Expectations and reality

Typical teens	Teens with ASD
Puberty period (ages 11–17)	*Puberty period* (ages 11–17)
period of rapid brain growth	period of rapid brain growth

Expectations

Physical bodily changes, such as hair growth, breast and muscle development, and the defining of the female or male form.

More responsibility; more maturity; more independence; more sociability.

Reality	*Reality*
Less maturity; increased drive for independence; less social awareness; compensatory joining of oneself to other group/club/gang.	Rapid brain growth will result in creating disconnection for a while increasing likelihood of increased frustration, lessened sensitivity towards others and some decreased awareness of the emotional states of others.

For both groups there appears to be a regression of skills and sensitivities that were acquired during childhood years.

Conclusion

Increased difficulties for both groups but heightened disconnection for teens with ASD due to increased focus but loss of connection and no additional channels to make up for this, e.g. joining social clubs or gangs may not occur.

If, however, we would like a partner and are unsure how to go about exploring this, then we need to consider all the earlier options from Chapter 2. Just because we are gay, bi or transsexual doesn't mean that we will need other methods to locate possible suitors. All the 'ways and means' that heterosexual individuals use are available to us. The only distinction between the two is our gender orientation. So we need to visit clubs for gays, bis or trannies. We need to move in the world that we belong to most. If we use the internet for this, we just need to be sure that it is legitimate. Check things out with someone you trust and don't go into anything you are unsure about.

Stress and anxiety

The Australian Bureau of Statistics (www.statistics.gov.au) reported in 2003 that 3–13 per cent of the typical population suffer with stress and anxiety. According to the Anxiety Disorders Association of America (www.adaa.org), anxiety disorders are the most common mental illness in the US with 19.1 million (13.3%) of the adult population (ages 18–54) affected. This isn't good news for lots and lots of people. However, prevalence for stress and anxiety for those of us on the autistic spectrum is 20–40 per cent (Carol 2003). Why is this so?

As individuals with ASD, although we grow up just like other people, we are not the same as other people. Our different way of understanding the world (as illustrated at the beginning of this book) will cause high stress levels for all of us and for those associated with us. Surely, if we want our relationships and our own self-confidence to be good then we need to develop a healthy acceptance of who we are. Much of our stress is related to an overwhelming sense that we are failures and will not be able to succeed at life in general. This does not have to be the case. For a very long time I believed I was a hopeless case. 'How could anyone love me?' I just wanted one person to walk beside me and accept me for who I was. In some ways though this could happen in my life once I had first learnt to accept myself.

Today, in this world of instant everything, it's not an easy task. It will take time and energy from each of us. I can only echo that time spent on building a positive image of one's self will pay off in the end. Take time to be amongst others who love and accept you for who you are. Avoid those people who don't. Take time to get involved with pursuits and relationships that give you a sense of fulfilment. Although you might not feel as if you have, you do have a choice here. So many of us have found 'life' and are enjoying being who we are amongst others who recognize our virtues. We are family, come join us.

CHAPTER 6

Making It Work

Family backgrounds

Real family

Families are interesting entities that consist of individuals who didn't necessarily choose each other. I like the poster that says 'You can choose your friends but you can't choose your relatives.' I like this poster because it implies that even if I don't always relate well to my family, I've got a second chance with my friends. I can tolerate family members even when I don't like them. I can attend family functions, because they are for 'family', but I might do so out of a sense of duty as opposed to really wanting to be there. I want to say at this point that I am very fortunate with my family. I have an extended family network who are very supportive and accepting of who I am. I love them and appreciate them. However, I know that this is not the case for so many others who feel controlled and dominated by 'family' and feel trapped.

I have many aunts and uncles on both my maternal and paternal sides of the family. When I was a youngster and going through a tough time, my parents sent me for several months to stay with my aunt. I remember the old guesthouse Aunty Bett ran and how the sounds echoed in the walls of the building. On another occasion when I was just five years old it was my maternal grandmother who recognized my 'special' ability in relating to animals. She gave me a kitten for my birthday. My cousins were always pleased to see me, even though I was known for my 'strange ways'. 'Oh that's just Wendy,' they would say as I mashed up all the food on my plate so as to disguise the variety of textures. I've always had problems with food that differed in texture and yet was served along together. For example, hot potatoes with cold salad; string beans and pasta; and fruit with bread and butter. I learnt that in order to be able to consume such food it was best to mix it all up and not 'see' the differences any more. This is still the way I eat food today. Only 'family' can be so accommodating!

Aunt Joan and Uncle Bob didn't raise children of their own; they were very special to us because they lived adventurous lives! Aunty always seemed young and full of exciting stories. Uncle always had silly jokes and tales to tell us. The following poem was read out at Uncle's funeral.

Joan and Bob

Joan and Bob
Bound together
For always and ever,
Like Scottish heather.
Bob's gone on ahead,
It was his time.
It isn't yours
And it isn't mine.

But his humour
He leaves us.
His 'och' and his 'ay'.
They never leave us
For memories can't die.

They live in our hearts,
The words that he spoke.
For he really was
Such a likeable bloke.

Death is only the winter at noon.
All comes to life again.
The spring will come soon.
Though winter is cold,
And lonely for some,
We've his love in our hearts,
This will keep our souls warm.

This poem serves to remind me of just how fragile we, and life, can be; with us as mere mortals, living and dying, and the world still spinning upon its axis. Family should be those others whom we can depend upon when others let us down. Some families are not blood-related. Nevertheless, they are 'family' just the same. What makes a family? I reckon love makes a family.

What baggage are we carrying?

'Baggage' is the term used to describe the attitudes, influences and beliefs and unresolved issues that we acquire over time as we travel through life. None of us experience things in the same way; therefore, we are affected differently by our life encounters. This might mean that we have different attitudes, beliefs and expectations about things to those of our partners. Potentially this can be a cause of conflict if it isn't understood and accounted for.

For example, some of us come from 'close-knit' families where family is the centre of things and where communication between individuals is a very frequent occurrence. Others of us come from families where we all eat at different times and none of us has a clue what might be happening for the other. These two extremes are not unusual and the families that operate like these are quite used to one another. But what will happen if we come from one family 'type' and our partner comes from the other?

Another form of baggage can be our own expectations of either our partners or ourselves. Expectation often disguises itself in the form of 'rights'. I once came across a saying that illustrated our thought patterns of expectation; it goes like this: It's right, it's my right, it's all right.' The problem with this though is that it might be 'right' for you but it might not be right for someone else. This means that even if it's right for you, it's not necessarily *all* right!

Are you coming at Christmas?

Those families that have been used to relating with one another often and are very much 'in and out' of each other's lives, might never have missed celebrating a festive season or holiday together. It might be assumed that 'of course we will go to my Mum's for Christmas'. The difficulty might not immediately present itself, but down the track a few years, one's partner or one's partner's family might feel left out and request that you go to them for Christmas. One partner might have been used to having Mum as a frequent visitor to their home; one partner may have been used to Mum doing all the washing or cooking all the meals, and so on, whilst the other partner is more likely to have left home and only had minimal contact with their family.

The sort of problems this might lead to are difficulties with partners understanding their respective families and how or why they function the way that they do. The families we each come from have contributed to the thinking patterns and attitudes we have. It's often quite difficult to understand one way of family relating if you come from a different type of family. Unfortunately, we might also believe that 'our family's way' of doing things is best, and this belief implies that our partner's family way of doing things is not so good! Usually, even if you don't come from a close-knit family, you will still defend and support the family network you come from. If you have to be on the defensive all the time about your family, then this will cause conflict between you and your partner. The good news is that if we can accept each other's 'family styles' and understand the influence that has upon our partners, we won't need to feel 'defensive', but we will need to sort out an agenda that suits us all.

For example, sometimes one's family might be upset when we say 'Oh, can't make it to Christmas dinner this year, but we can come for the New Year' or something like this. We need to make sure that our own partnerships are paramount in any decision we make and our 'families' come second. Learning to put our partner and our own immediate family's needs first is the best foundation for building a successful marriage. If we allow our parents and parents-in-law to dictate to us how we, as a separate unit, should live, we can expect to have 'the baggage' we bring with us weigh us down and even stop our relationship from growing.

Spring cleaning

Every now and then we need to dust down our relationships and breathe new life into them. Sometimes clearing away the debris and the muck that builds up over time can be quite revealing. If we want to maintain that 'just like new' look and see our image reflected in the polished wood, then we do have to pay it some attention. The muck and rubbish I speak about might be relational discord or the trash that creeps in and stifles out the light. It might be that we allow anger or frustration to build up in our relationships, which can separate us from truly caring for and loving our partner. It also stops us from receiving love too. Give yourself some time to do some relational stock taking. If you find yourself short on the love and affection you once felt for your partner, ask yourself if it's because you need to clear out the channels of communication and get a few matters accounted for.

You might find that your partner holds a bag of grievances too, and by sitting down to talk together you can both face up to your wounds. Damage that is not repaired quickly can degenerate and worsen over time. Sometimes, because it's been ignored and no one has paid heed to it, it might be beyond repair. To stop this happening it's best to attend to things quickly, before they get too bad. One way to do this is to have regular time for chatting about things. In my relationship I refuse to let the sun go down on my anger. This means that I won't go to bed with my partner until we have sorted out the things that irk us and have dealt with them.

It's important to me!

Recognizing when something is important to another person can be quite difficult if we don't have a sense of this for ourselves. It might be a particular routine (e.g. the way one hangs out the washing or the way one squeezes the toothpaste tube), time for sleeping or supper requirements, the way something is presented (e.g. a meal or how the shopping is unpacked), particular items of clothing, particular programmes on the television or even a particular greeting at a particular time. I have needed to learn that when something is of specific importance for my partner, I need to value it too. Of course, there are times when I don't see the sense in this, feel the need for it or agree with my partner's experience. But, this isn't relevant to the issue. The important point here is that I respect my partner and what's of value to them. This is also true for ourselves, and we too will have things that are important to us.

Learning how to 'allow' these things to coexist and not cause conflict isn't easy. I love to watch *Star Trek* and most science fiction programmes on the TV. I also love nature programmes and history documentaries. My partner prefers drama and romance! How do we accommodate these differences? The first thing we need to understand is that having different likes and dislikes is OK. We are all different and it's quite usual to have some things in common and others that are of specific interest to one partner but not to the other. Recognizing and accepting this is the first step. The next step is to work out a way of accommodating the needs for both of us. When my partner is watching a programme that doesn't interest me, I have some options. I can sit and watch it too, if my partner likes to have the company. I can read a book as my partner watches, or I can occupy my time in a pursuit that I choose. Sometimes in our house we tape programmes for one of us so that we can watch them when the other is busy. I'm still not always comfortable with watching a programme alone and having my partner somewhere else doing something else because my programmes don't interest them. But it's only the programme that they are not interested in, they are still interested in me! I can live with this.

Couple identity

Just as it is important to have a sense of 'self', it is also true that we need a sense of couple-ness. When I was first married, I didn't recognize that I needed to take into consideration the needs, wants and desires of my husband. I was used to making my own decisions without consultation with others. I was also used to using my time in the way that suited me. During the first year of married life I still lived as if I were single. I went off on journeys, hitchhiked around the countryside, took myself off to visit friends or stay places that were of interest to me. It didn't occur to me that this would upset or offend my partner. I didn't consult with him about this or check in on how he felt about it. At times he would come home from work to find a note saying 'Gone away for a while, see you when I get back.' Today, however, I do recognize that this wasn't the most appropriate behaviour, and now I check in regularly with my partner!

As a couple, you will have certain shared values and concerns. As a couple, you might feel that you 'fit together' and make a great team. Each of you brings something of value to your relationship that is unique and special. This special ingredient is you. I remember spending ages over how to finish off a letter that was an invitation for friends to come to dinner. Should I end this letter with my name first or should I use my partner's name? This dilemma was so strong that I was unable to complete the invitation! In reality there is no rule about this, each or either is allowed to go first and as a couple you might like the way your names sound in a particular format or you might not care. Whichever way we choose, we are still a couple and neither is of more importance than the other, we are equals.

Being an equal partner in any relationship will mean having equal responsibilities. Sometimes, although we might recognize this academically, we may fail to put it into practice. We might have particular expectations from our partner that concern home duties or particular duties outside the home. Probably the best thing to do is to discuss our expectations with our partners, just to check in that these are their expectations also and that each is happy with their expected role. I know some couples where the division of labour is what we might call 'typical', that is the woman takes on the domestic duties and leaves the wood chopping and accounts to her male partner. I know some couples who have separate bank accounts and some who share bank accounts. I know some couples where the male is happier with domestic duties and leaves the paying of accounts to his female counterpart. Partnership is all about sharing out the responsibilities in the way that allows for the full development of our skills and self-confidence. Our skills may not always fit in with typical expectation, and we may actually be better at those things often thought of as 'not typical' for our particular gender. As long as our choices suit us, and we as a team and partnership are happy, this is what counts.

Have you ever looked at a couple or family passing by and noted that the family dog seems to resemble the family? I have seen a boxer dog at play with its owner and they really did seem to have many features in common. The same can be said of a spaniel, terrier or Great Dane! Why is this so? Identity reflects who we are and sometimes this extends to those other things that are important to us. This might be our pets, our car or our mobile phone! Other people pick up on who we are and what they might expect from us by noticing these things. You might hear them say, 'Oh he's the sporty kind' or 'You can tell she keeps a tidy home', and so on. This isn't a bad thing, but we do need to be careful that we don't always judge things by their outward appearance. I think people do this because they need a 'handle' on what to expect and what it might mean for them. If this isn't forthcoming in any practical sense, then they judge from what is available to them. Usually the most available information is that which we take in through our senses; sight is one of the first senses to give us a picture of what we are experiencing from others.

Who I am and who you are will be connected to our choice of clothing, TV programmes, diet, recreational activity, hopes, dreams and chosen occupation. When we join forces and become a couple, a family, then we pool all of who we are and all of what we bring with us. Although we often look on the outside to give us a picture of what's on the inside, this can be deceiving and may give us the wrong picture. We need to look further and spend some time uncovering what might be happening on the inside for each of us.

On the inside

On the inside of who we are there are lots of emotions, experiences and belief systems that maintain the essence of our being. We will operate from these even if it's subconsciously and we are unaware of it. It is these inner belief systems that colour the way we see the world and the way we see our relationships. For example, if our partner is focused upon some activity, issue or event, and this takes up their attention, we might conclude that we are no longer important to them and this can give rise to conflict. The reality might be, however, that because we are important to them and they feel safe with us, they may feel free to be themselves and pursue their interests. Personal autonomy is a precious commodity, and once gained serves to set others free. It's not that we don't want to give our partners space to be themselves or that we don't recognize the need for couple or family time, but it is to do with how we feel about ourselves. If this is good, we tend to be in a place that allows others the freedom to grow and express themselves. If it isn't so good, we may be looking to our relationships to prop up our sense of value, expecting always to be the centre of someone else's world. If the latter is true for you I think you can expect more conflict in your relationships than if the former is true.

Belief systems are powerful things that dictate to our emotions and our thoughts. Sometimes these are positive (e.g. 'You are a worthwhile person') and sometimes they are negative (e.g. 'You are worthless'). If we see ourselves as a person with little value then, as well as 'putting ourselves down', we will also allow others to abuse and use us. If we see ourselves as individuals of value, we will take better care of ourselves, and we won't tolerate abusive behaviour towards ourselves from others. Because our self-image has a powerful impact upon what we expect from ourselves and from others, our relationships stand a better chance of succeeding if we value the person we are. It's also easier to respect and value another person when we value ourselves.

If we want our relationship to grow and develop into a sustaining healthy entity, it needs to be planted in ground that is healthy, nourishing and supportive. For example, if we notice that the weeds are getting a bit too close for comfort and they are choking the plants in our garden, then we pull those weeds out. It's the same for our relationships. The types of weeds that choke our relationships usually come disguised as other things, and we may not realize they are weeds. For instance, what about gossip and hearsay? 'There's no smoke without fire' I hear people say. But actually this may not be true. Gossip and stories about the actions of another person may be founded in fantasy or in reality. It's not the ground they come from that is the problem, it's the idea of what they might grow into that is of concern! I choose to believe good things about my partner and I choose to check in with them about anything else that blocks my thinking of good things about them. This way I get the opportunity to share what's on my mind and they get the opportunity to speak to me from their perspective. If I listen to the gossip of others, which might be given to me second or third hand, then I am only fuelling negative and damaging concepts that feed paranoia and discontent.

There is a 'you', there is a 'me' and there is an 'us'. For the 'us' to be confident and good, we each need the developing autonomy that comes from the healthy esteem of each other as separate people. Maintaining self-confidence and confidence in our relationships go hand in hand.

The Tree of Life

I am a seed hidden in a very dark place.
I am a seed designed to seek the sun's face.
I am a seed, to grow I need space.
I am a seed. I am a seed.

I am a sapling reaching for the rain.
I am a sapling with stems that need to train.
I am a sapling whose buds will sprout again.
I am a sapling. I am a sapling.

I am a tree with branches tall and wide.
I am a tree where birds can safely hide.
I am a tree whose seeds I will provide.
I am a tree. I am a tree.

We each have a place in the world that we are a part of. We each want others to share particular aspects of who we are, where we are going and what we hope the future will open up for us. I don't want to stay hidden in a dark place; I want to be a tree that can grow and develop in a sunny, warm place where I'll have plenty of nourishment. Relationships can be like tall healthy trees that provide us with shelter, food and a home to rest in, or they can be prickly bushes that irritate us and block our paths – painful obstacles that get in our way. Only you know what kind of relationship you are in. Only you can choose what you want from life. Others can direct us and assist us but they can't live our lives for us. Families can be safe havens or they can be traps that suffocate and frustrate the lives of their members.

Staying sane

Staying sane when things don't work out for us or when we seem submerged in misunderstanding is quite difficult. When I feel a sense of injustice or when it's difficult to appreciate the other person's perspective, I want to take the other individuals involved in my discomfort and make them 'see' things as I do. I want them to agree with my thinking and share my experience. Of course, they might not be able to do or be what I think they should, and I need to realize that other people have their own mind and their own way of doing things, which might be quite different to mine. But knowing this academically and being able to put it into practice are two different things.

So, although it can seem like hard work learning to accept ourselves for who we are and our partners for who they are, it's necessary work that reaps lots of welcome reward. It might mean that even when I feel discomfort at the knowledge that someone does not agree with me or see things the way I do, I can choose to accept them and choose not to react to my feelings. This means that I acknowledge my discomfort and put up with it. It will pass and things will calm down. I am allowed to have my view and my partner is allowed to have theirs. It's uncomfortable, but it won't kill me.

Staying sane also requires us to acknowledge that because we are different people, we may have different tastes in recreational activities, friends and family matters. At times, due to the constant battle with this, we might think and feel like we are going crazy. In all of our working relationships, activities and chosen occupations we will need time off. Time for relaxation and recreation are essential to the well-being of any relationship. If one stays inside the house or the office all the time and doesn't go outside, the opportunity to extend one's horizons and note that there is a world to explore out there can be missed. I love to walk, even when it's just around my neighbourhood. I pass other homes that look different to mine, whose gardens, fences and walls are different to mine. Sometimes I pass blocks of flats and sometimes I pass larger single homes that look like mansions in comparison. Then there are the dogs that pass by and we get to exchange greetings. The best thing about being outside, though, are the birds I get to see! Flying high or low around me are birds of all different types. I once read a book called *Jonathan Livingston Seagull* by Richard Bach. It was all about a common seagull that had a vision; who decided to explore how he could be all he wanted to be and more! Whenever I see the birds that fly around me I am reminded of this story and I feel inspired again. Instead of focusing upon my difficulties and feeling overwhelmed, I can take time to put things into perspective – time to realize that we all have difficult times and that these times help fashion our lives into being what we want them to be. 'No pain no gain', as someone once said to me. Of course, this doesn't mean that we have to experience pain and cause pain to others before we gain understanding. It's just a saying that is meant to help us cope with the difficulties we experience and understand the reality that such pain is fleeting and doesn't need to be everlasting.

CHAPTER 7

Building a Safe Place

Feeling 'at home' in our relationships

What is our place?

Each of us has 'a place' – a place where we belong and where we can be ourselves. But it isn't always possible just to be ourselves, especially when we are amongst other people. Appreciating that some people will support us in who we are and some will not is quite a difficult lesson to learn. The package we present in can take us years to achieve, and, as adults, we will be pretty well established. The personality we are born with, the attributes that genetically determine our temperament, our looks, hobbies, desires, wants and needs, will vary according to who we are and where we have come from. It's not just the country we were born in or the culture we grew up in that determines our character, but our genes have a big part to play too. I'm not entering into the nature versus nurture debate here, just stating the facts. We each are a combination of both of these; they work hand in hand. So, what can I be responsible for? Do I choose my life direction now as an adult or do I believe it is already predetermined and I cannot do anything about the things that happen to me? Well, maybe choice has a bigger role to play than we had imagined? I may not have had control over who my parents were or where I grew up, but I can take control over many of my decisions and choices now, as an adult.

Can you say that the relationships you are involved in today are safe places for you? There once was a time when it seemed the individuals I was drawn to relate to were not the ideal people for Wendy. They were not accepting of who she was, nor did they encourage her in her evolving lifestyle. It's a bit like other things that we find ourselves doing. For example, have you ever chosen an outfit that looked great on the shop dummy in the shop window, but when you got home and tried it on it didn't fit you in the same way? Sometimes our friendships can be like this. We think a certain individual will make a great friend and be really supportive of who we are, but when it comes down to it, they will only support us if our ideas and experiences mirror theirs. A true friend will travel with us in all of our adventures, and even when they don't agree with our choices they will support us just the same. A rhyme that has sustained me in times of doubt is: 'A friend will go anywhere with you, a friend takes the good with the bad. The times that I have with my good friend, are the best times that I ever had.'

Having friends and family can be the very best thing, but only if they are safe places where we can be ourselves. 'Make yourself at home' someone says. Then, as you open the fridge and help yourself to 'dinner' the same person can feel that they have been taken advantage of. Why do some people say things that they don't mean? Why do they seem supportive until you need them? I don't know the answer to this, I only know it happens. The thing to do is aim to check in on what people actually mean when they say these things and try to sort out the differences between 'being nice', 'being friendly' and 'being home from home'.

Today I choose to surround myself with individuals who accept me for me, and wherever possible I avoid being amongst people who do not. Living our lives to please and appease others only drains the life from us and will leave us feeling dejected and worthless. This doesn't mean that we won't want to do things that please others, but it does mean that this concept doesn't need to rule our relationships. In an ideal world relationships and family are built upon mutual respect and understanding. This isn't always everyone's experience though and, unfortunately, we don't live in an ideal world. However, if each of us understands this and commits to working positively on our own relationships, things can change for the better, for us.

Discovering 'our place' in the world and uncovering where we fit best is no easy task. Some of us like our home to look a certain way. For example, we choose colours and furnishings that reflect the things we like to have around us. What happens when one of us likes certain décor and the other likes something different? The art of negotiating was probably born out of similar conflicts! Relationship isn't just about having the 'right' prints on the wall and relating to the 'right' people. These superficial things have a place in the overall scheme of things perhaps, but they are not sufficient in themselves to maintain a healthy relationship. Relationships need substance, and that substance is based upon my feeling 'at home' with my partner and the safety that we share together. Whether we are in our own home or the home of those we are in a relationship with, we should be able to relax and know that, just as we are, we are accepted.

ASD: My Gender

My gender and I are a package.
We come as part of the deal.
'But ASD shows far more damage.
Look at the things that you feel.'

I cannot account for these feelings,
Emotions intense and extreme.
But my issues with everyday dealings
Can cause me to rant, shout and scream.
I don't desire the 'make-up'.
Fashion and high-heels don't appeal.
I don't like perfume or my hair cut,
But my need for 'understanding' is real.

The expectations placed upon me,
Being female and all,
Push me further into pain and grief,
With my back against the wall.

'I cannot multi-task,' I say.
'But you must, You're a woman. You can.'
You must cook, clean, organize and play
The role that supports your man.'

'Your children and men depend on you,
You must be strong, in control and sure.'

'What if these things I cannot do?
What if my timing is poor?'

'You must work harder, try harder to be,
What society says and dictates.'
'But both my ASD and gender are me, you see
They both influence my states.'

As a woman I function differently.
As a woman I think, see and feel.
As a woman I value *all* that is me.
My ASD is part of the deal.

I have been asked the question 'If there was a cure for ASD tomorrow, would you take it?' For me, the answer would be 'no'. I acknowledge that my ASD can get in the way of many things that I wish were different: it interferes with my comprehension of social situations and it seems to be something others pick up on and 'judge' me for. However, it also allows me to access life in a way that many others who are not on the ASD spectrum cannot. It gives me the 'edge' and sharpens my senses, enabling me to enjoy my passion for birds, for example. I have come to understand that typical individuals have their problems too. For many of them the social arena is a nightmare and they wish that the pressures upon them to perform, fit in, have the 'right' car, clothes, house, job, and so on, would cease! It must take up an enormous amount of energy and brain space to fulfil the requirements of being a typical individual! I'll keep my ASD, thank you! Having said this, though, I know individuals with ASD who would be first in the queue for a cure.

Empathy

Quite often when one reads the literature about ASD, it will say that people with ASD lack empathy. Empathy is a word given to define the ability to feel for and connect with what's happening for another person. In my experience, and also what I have observed in other individuals with ASD, it just isn't true to say that we lack empathy. What I think might be happening, though, is that our empathy relates to our own attachments and is not so accessible outside of attachment. In other words, it's much easier to have empathy for what or who we're attached to than it is when we can't connect. This is showing us that it's not the lack of the facility for empathy but the medium through which we experience it that might be different, between those of us with ASD and those of us without. Due to our monotropic disposition, those of us with ASD may even experience too much empathy. By this I mean the intensity of our feelings can be really strong and almost out of proportion to the reality. Sometimes when I've heard a story about the pain and suffering an individual has experienced, I find myself in floods of tears with the emotion of feeling their sense of injustice. When this happens to me, it's usually connected to the injustice I myself have experienced. On another occasion, I may hear of a different individual going through a hard time, but my emotional response can be nil even though intellectually I can appreciate what they are going through. I think this happens to us because, with one individual I could identify with their pain, and with the other I could not. This might mean, within the context of our relationships, we can share some of the distress and difficulty our partner might go through, but at other times we can't identify at all. To me, this understanding was quite revolutionary and helped me to understand why at times my partner seemed to connect to my difficulties and at other times seemed completely insensitive to them. If this is happening for you in your relationships, it's probably a good idea to talk about it together. This way, you can explore what you understand of one another's issues, and, it is hoped, resolve them.

The lovely thing about understanding one another is that it releases you from expectation. I no longer expect my partner to pick up on all of the difficulties I'm experiencing. However, I can tell my partner what's happening for me and this allows them to respond to me appropriately. Non-ASD people usually read the signs that other people give out to them, and this lets them know what's going on for that person. This is called mind reading. The reality is, nobody reads anybody else's mind; all they can do is read the signs. For those of us with ASD, because our attention might not be on the signs that a person is giving out (due to our difficulty with reading body language and facial expressions), we need to tell one another and paint the picture more clearly.

Do we share everything?

Knowing that sharing is a very good thing, and that being able to share our hearts and minds with another person is a good thing, we could easily believe that we have to share everything. The reality is, though, that if we disclose everything about who *we* are, what *we* think, and don't pay enough attention to what the other person is experiencing, we may give the impression of being selfish. The other important factor to note is that it's not always necessary or even beneficial to tell somebody everything that's going on for us. Sometimes we can have experiences or opinions that remain ours alone, that are not necessary to share with another. For example, a friend's choice of clothing or their hairstyle or their chosen recreational activity might not be what you would choose for yourself. If you were, however, to tell them your opinion that the clothes, hairstyle or recreational activity were boring or not to your taste, you could alienate them. The good news about being in a relationship is that we can accept those things about the other that are not always comfortable or in line with our own choices. This means we are free to be ourselves and our partners are free to be themselves.

Relationships that are founded on truthfulness and honesty might seem like a good thing. In essence they certainly are, but at times our partners might not want us to be honest when it comes to making them feel good about who they are. For example, our partner might ask, 'Do I look all right?' and you might think what they're wearing doesn't do them justice and they look hideous, but it would be more appropriate to say, 'You look lovely, darling, but maybe the other shirt works better.'

The other aspect to telling your partner all your thoughts and feelings might mean that they feel overrun with your experiences and there's no room for their own, so we need to check in with our partners that we're not being too overwhelming. Recently, I had an experience that led me to a situation where I knew to be truthful would hurt my partner. Not only would it hurt my partner, but it might even damage our relationship. When I talked about this situation to my good friend, they helped me to understand that to withhold information was not always a bad thing. I felt that not to tell my partner meant I was lying to them and this was a very uncomfortable experience. But when my friend asked, 'Why do you want to tell them? Is it to make you feel good or is it to make them feel good?' I quickly realized the reason behind the need to tell my partner was to make me feel good. This understanding has helped me to identify that there are times when it is better not to tell. So even though not voicing the things that were on my mind felt uncomfortable, it was more a matter of discerning what needed to be said and what didn't. We might need to practise this understanding in order to become more at home in it.

Looking after our self

Where did I go?

During the time that I was married and my children were still young I experienced times when my life was so taken up with 'family life' that I didn't seem to have any time for myself. Although I had times when I met with friends or times when I was away from the family, these were still times when family matters reigned. It wasn't until my youngest son was eight years old that I thought about rediscovering 'me'. For Wendy that meant going back to school and starting on a programme of continuing education that opened the door to university.

Maybe you are feeling that you don't have a life of your own any more? Maybe you are wondering how to get back some sense of personal identity that is not referred to via your title or your family? When we were involved with a workshop recently each of us had to introduce ourselves and say who we were and what we did. It was interesting to note how many of us introduced ourselves as being the wife of... or the mother of..., and so on. So, what happened to the person who existed before they were a wife or a mother? Is our identity only bound up in and through how we relate to our spouse or offspring? If it is, we might find ourselves feeling quite lost when our children leave home or our partner dies. The better option is to keep the 'me' alive and refuse to get bogged down beneath the weight of family woe!

How do we do this? Well I guess that it will depend upon what interests you and what you feel drawn to. I wanted to further my education and I joined classes that I was interested in. You might want to do the same or you might prefer to join a club or a society. Some of my friends have obtained the type of employment that allows them to work and maintain their family lives as well. Whatever you choose to do, the important thing is that it suits you and your situation.

Being part of a community that relates to us outside of our families can open up new dimensions for us. We can experience encouragement and mutual interests that breathe new life into our situations. It's great too to have interesting conversations with other adults that aren't just about the problems of our children's education or puberty! Rather, we bring our own desires, needs, wants and interests into direct contact with other adults, which can be a refreshing and nurturing time for our own self-esteem.

Autonomy

Having a sense of self that accommodates who we are and allows for interaction with others is great. But what do we do when the relationships we have known and enjoyed change, or even end (due to our moving house, state or country, or our friends moving away or losing touch with us)? If our sense of 'Life' is based upon interaction with others and then those others leave, we might feel bereft. It certainly seems to be the case for those of us who retire from employment that gave us the sense of who we were. Retirement is offered up as that time in our lives when we can relax and enjoy the time in recreation and chosen activities, instead of in work. Well, the reality is that our work might be the avenue that we take where self-fulfilment is the outcome, and once removed from that source of fulfilment we again feel quite lost.

So, if these things are happening for you and you feel in some kind of fog that just won't lift, what can you do about it? I think we have several options, and this is good news. Some people I know have gone back to working as volunteers for agencies that rely upon them to do the jobs they do (Red Cross; Home Help; Community Networks, to name but a few). Others have taken up gardening, returned to study, joined their local library group, walking group, and so on. It's OK to need other people in your life and I think most of us are created to be interdependent, not independent. When I first left England and moved to Australia, some individuals told me that I needed to start a new life and that I should leave my 'old life' behind me. They said that I should make new friends in my new country and say goodbye to my existing friends. I felt really uncomfortable with their advice and very sad at the thought of leaving my friends and of not communicating with them ever again. Now I realize that although these people were trying to be helpful, they were not giving me the right advice, and it's perfectly OK to stay relating to your friends, even if you move countries.

Some of my friends live in different countries to me but we stay in contact via email or phone, and I even get to catch up with them in person from time to time. Although it's a great idea to have friends that live close by, it doesn't have to only be that way. The internet can be a great source of information and allow us to connect to a wealth of understanding that might help us through some rough times. We can also find others 'on-line' in chat rooms that we can join. There are so many other people around the world that are experiencing similar things to ourselves and we can share with one another rather than travelling through our difficulties on our own.

How to have a good argument

I used to believe that arguing was wrong and good communication meant always being agreeable, but now I appreciate that there is such a thing as a 'good' argument. Having disagreements and learning how to express these appropriately is healthy. If we bottle things up inside of us, we could be building towards an explosive occasion that we might regret. So, dealing with events and situations that cause us discomfort, as they arise, is a better option. 'OK, Wendy, I agree with this, but how do I do it?' I know that for some of us with ASD, recognizing that we need to act upon something might take us a bit of time. That is, we are involved with conversation, but we don't necessarily process the information quickly enough to respond straight away. I think the thing to do is talk about this with our partner, or with whomever the other person is that we are involved with, when we are not having a disagreement. As a way of discovering about each other we can share with others that we need time to process information. Then, when an occasion occurs and we realize afterwards that we are not happy, but that we were unable to process this at the time, we can let the person know. Because we have already told them that this is what happens to us, it won't come as a surprise. Another thing that might be helpful here is checking in on a regular basis that we are keeping up with a conversation and that we have an understanding of what's going on. I frequently ask others to slow the pace down and converse more slowly so I can follow. I also check in with what I've understood, just to be sure that we are all on the same track!

If you have been involved with a dispute and you feel a sense of injustice about something, you might feel a bit 'shaky' and uncomfortable. You might want to 'fix' the situation and make someone see your viewpoint. This can be a very strong feeling, and one that can completely dominate our thinking. I have gone through a number of battles like this and have come out the other side feeling torn apart by storms that have raged out of control. Now, I try to recognize those battles that I have a chance of winning or surviving, and those I know I will lose. Some storms are worth weathering, but there are others that we need to avoid. Recognizing the difference between them can take a bit of experience! Relationships can be like ships in the night. Having the right equipment to navigate stormy waters in the dark can make the difference between safe arrival at port or being lost at sea. The sort of equipment needed to ride out a relationship storm may consist of the following: maps for navigating emotions; the life jacket of diplomacy for self-protection; a lifeboat of willingness to apologize, even if you don't believe you are at fault; and positive words of encouragement to sustain you whilst waiting for rescue.

CHAPTER 8

Maintaining Our Safe Place

Communication

When I have asked people what they think speech is used for they usually reply 'for communication'. Of course they might be right, but all too often speech doesn't really communicate what we want it to. There are many reasons for this. It might be that we cannot locate the right words, or that we haven't had the time to process what we want to say. At times it's only after an event that I realize what I could or should have said! I can feel really cross with myself and wish that I didn't take so long to work things out and to connect with a situation. Maybe this happens to you too and your experiences are like mine? What can we do about it? I think the first thing we need to do is to recognize that we need more time to process conversation than some other people. If we know this we can then let those significant others know too. Our partners might be relieved to know this, because they might have thought that we were ignoring them when really we are taking our time to consider how to answer them. Also, if our partners know this is happening for us, they have the opportunity to think more before they speak, so they can put what they want to say into words more accessible for us, and they can allow us more time to reply than they themselves might need.

Taking our time to process words that we hear can be a very good thing, because we've taken time to think. This can mean that our responses are more intelligent and more thoughtful. I actually think that at times speech is cheap, and even though there are people who can talk easily and fast, it doesn't mean that their speech is of a better quality than ours. Also, taking time to think before responding allows our heads to catch up with our hearts. For example, if we are quick to respond to an emotive situation, our responses might be more emotional than they are thoughtful. When we've had time to process the emotional event with a bit of distance between it and us, we might be able to respond more appropriately. Sometimes in situations in my relationships where I have spoken before I thought, I have really regretted the words that have come out of my mouth.

Recognizing that we are all different people with our own belief systems and ways of communicating would be helpful in learning how to read each other well. For some of us, our negative self-esteem might cause us to doubt our confidence in our relationships. For example, if we don't feel as intelligent or as knowledgeable as the person we are communicating with, we may feel inferior or even that we have not got a valid point of view. This can lead into the belief that we are not likeable people and that we fail at whatever we do. However, needing time to process language and consider our replies only means that we need more time, and this may mean that we are more reflective in our communication, not that we are a failure.

Sometimes, because of our need to slow down and think about our replies, we may feel pressured by a need to respond quickly. This might mean we promise things that we can't deliver on, or that we say things that, when we've had time to think, we don't really mean. Our partners might then feel misled and believe that we have made promises that we then break. This leads them to conclude something about who we are as people, which may not be accurate. What I am beginning to realize is that a person who can seem moody and changeable may actually be a person who has responded before they have had time to process the communication. When they have had time to think things through, they may reach a different conclusion to the one previously given. This would mean that it's not so much that they are changing their mind or breaking a promise, but that the earlier response was given in haste, and now they've had time to evaluate the situation, their response might be different.

Let's communicate

Recognizing our communication style (whether we use lots of speech, little speech, body language, facial expressions, or all or none of these) is the first step to being a good communicator. The next step is understanding the communication style of the significant others in our lives. Then we need to work out what the important information to communicate is: what is superficial, what is important, and which bits need to be skipped. When we can do these things it is more likely we will be more confident in expressing the things that we are thinking and feeling.

Cultural differences between backgrounds can also impact on how we communicate. Usually, using 'I' statements in our conversation (e.g. 'I think', 'I feel') are good ways to convey what's going on for us without causing the other person to feel threatened. However, some people, when we say 'I', may interpret this to mean we are superior to them and find this really threatening. Although it's good to avoid saying 'You should', 'You must' or 'You need to', it's still important to check in on our conversation with those we are relating to and confirm that the message they are receiving is the message we are intending to convey. For example, using 'you' phrases like the above can come across as accusing, and the individuals we relate to might feel that they then need to defend themselves. This can result in our going around in circles, feeling attacked, needing to defend ourselves, and so on; and the real things we want to communicate might not be understood.

Scenario 1

'We are going to eat out tonight. You should get changed and dress in more appropriate clothing.'

A better way to say this might be: 'We've been in our day clothes all day today; I want to change my clothes and put different clothes on when we go out to eat tonight, what will you be wearing?'

Scenario 2

'You should help me around the house.'

A better way to say this might be: 'I miss having you interact with me around the house. Let's explore a way where we can work together.'

Concepts

Sometimes we can have a concept about something that is inaccurate or incomplete, yet we might not know this and we may be living our lives subject to a misunderstanding. Concepts can be tricky things, everyone has them, but quite often our concepts don't match those of other people. If it so happens that our concepts don't match those of our partners, then we might be in for times of unnecessary conflict. Again it's really important that we check in with our partners to substantiate that our concept of a person, an event, an understanding, an expectation, and so on, is the same as theirs.

For years my partner and I (even though we loved each other very much) experienced times of conflict due to concepts we had about one another that were inaccurate. These beliefs we each held led us into particular thinking about the other that might go something like this:

> *Person 1:* 'If s/he really loved me, s/he would know that I need her/him to do that.'

> *Person 2:* 'If s/he really loved me, s/he would not be demanding this from me.'

Say Person 1 is an individual with Asperger's syndrome and attention deficit hyperactivity disorder (ADHD); this might mean they often need to be active and on the go. Their thought behind the belief that their partner should understand them might come from an incomplete understanding of their partner which might go something like this: 'S/he knows that I find this difficult; my need to be active is connected to my hyperactivity, it's so unfair to be expected to do and be what I am not.'

Person 2, unfortunately, might be coming from a belief system that is similar to Person 1. They might not have a full understanding either. The belief of either person might be based upon their assumption that the other person 'knows' where they are coming from and is deliberately acting out of their needs and desires. The reality might be though, that neither individual has a full picture of the other and they both might be misreading each other. Much conflict can result from misunderstanding the attention behind an action or a statement that

comes from another person. Each of us has our own agendas and belief systems that we operate from which can undermine our relationships if not checked.

One of the recent understandings that my partner and I have un-
covered about each other goes like this: 'Oh, that's what's happening.
The more stressed you are the faster you go. For me, it's the opposite.
The more stressed I am the slower I go.' This understanding that we
operate differently because we are made differently, released us from
the belief that said: 'I believed that you should do things the same
way as I do them. Because you do it differently, I believed you were
doing it wrong.' Since growing into and developing good foundations for any relationship depends upon knowing one another, accepting our differences and working with who we are, the above
understanding has allowed us to move on with more confidence in
our relating to one another.

Confidence

Being confident in our relationships and sure of each other because
we have the right information about one another is a small but
necessary part of communicating what and who we are. Another
aspect that helps build confidence and good communication is
knowing that we can safely be ourselves. For me as an individual with
ASD and ADHD, being understood and accepted for who I am has
been a huge hurdle in having confidence in my relationships.

For years I constantly checked in with my partner and lived with a
constant need for reassurance. Fortunately I have a partner who accommodates my need and understands my 'short-term' experiences.
By this I mean that the feelings I have connected to my experiences
are intermittent, fleeting, intense and constantly shifting. At times I
have little 'feeling' at all and operate from a collection of mechanical
responses. Having another person know and understand this about
me whilst accepting the person I am, frees me to be confident and sure
of many things associated with relating. If our partners are not relating to us from such understanding, then misunderstanding, miscon-
ception and, in fact, missing the point completely, might be the
constant centre of our relationships. Truly knowing one another

takes time and effort. It isn't an easy concept to master, but if we each accept this and commit to working on it we will have a better chance of succeeding in our relationships.

Knowing You, Knowing Me

Knowing that you know me
Makes me both glad and sad.
I want your full acceptance,
Don't want you feeling bad.

Because I am not perfect,
I'll upset you now and then.
The things that I just do not get,
Or the occasions when…

When I am most insensitive,
When I fail to see your need.
Knowing that you choose to give,
Even when I cannot read…

Read the signs you give me,
Read the needs you hold,
Knowing you forgive me,
Gives me time to be bold…

Bold in reaching out for you,
Bold in letting you reach in.
Together with our knowing,
Each new day we can begin…

Begin to grow and reach our dreams,
Begin to hold our heads up high.
Begin to reinforce those seams,
That hold the future for you and I.

How to let go of the past

When does the past begin?

It's easy to think of 'The Past' as only referring to things that happened long ago. Actually the past refers to any event that has already occurred. This might mean the past is just a few minutes ago. How good are you at holding on to the past? I know that I need some time to think things through and to process any event. I also need that time to be uncluttered and to be free from the added overload that more words or activities might bring. This is fine; we can accommodate that need. But, what if I still feel the feelings that went with the event? What if those feelings are uncomfortable and I can't shake them off? I just keep going over and over the same ground! Perhaps this happens for you too. It's certainly really difficult to move on in one's life when events and situations that have been hurtful or difficult just keep on replaying for us. Well, I've found the answer to this! I liken it to having an untidy room that needs attention. The room is full of clutter; dust and rubbish are all mixed up with the room's contents. One steps inside of the door and feels overwhelmed. 'I can't clear and clean that room,' I think. 'It's just too messy.' Well actually, Wendy, you can. You just have to go in there and make a start. Begin in one corner and work your way through to the next. It won't be comfortable and we might not feel like it, but that's the key you see. We don't have to feel like it, we just have to do it. The discomfort might hang around for a while, but eventually we will be able to go into that room and feel OK.

Bad memories

Memories are things that can haunt us, even in our dreams. When those memories are bad and cause us each time to revisit a particular event or situation, then it can mean we travel through all of the emotions again and again. This is very exhausting and very debilitating. Learning how to deal with past memories like these, so that they lose their power, isn't easy. One thing I know that I need to do, is not give my bad memories any fuel that might help to keep them alive. For example, I try not to feed them by thinking about them. I do my best to starve them in the hope that their hold over me will lessen.

'But the more I try not to think about them the more they fill my mind,' a friend says. Yes, I know that this can be true. Perhaps if we focus our thoughts on a different matter (an area of study, an interest, physical exercise, and so on) it might be helpful? One of my friends actively chose, even though it was the opposite to how she felt, to think negatively about a person she loved and focused on considering them as 'the enemy'. This helped my friend deal with unrequited love. She could have focused on how hurt she was and on the injustice of the situation. This would have increased her pain and been quite disabling. Choosing to shift her focus from self-pain to preservation was one of the positive steps forward for my friend.

Another way to deal with our past negative experiences is to see them as part of life's tapestry. In one way or another they can impact upon our lives for good. I find the scripture that says 'The enemy meant this for harm but the Lord means it for good' a helpful phrase. This isn't saying that the bad things that happen to us are good, but that we can use them for something positive. Maybe it's a bit like taking the waste and the rubbish of everyday life and using it as manure fertilizer to grow good things. I have lots of bad memories. Most of them are connected to the injustice of hurtful behaviour done to me by others. I have been abused, used and mistreated in a number of ways by individuals who were significant to me and whom I loved and cared for. Some of those individuals I still love and I miss today. I long for their acceptance and for their friendship. I could brood on this and feel sorry for myself, and this would keep the power over my life in their hands! When I realized that my discomfort and even anger for some of those past events was still ruling my life today, I also realized that those individuals involved in my past had no awareness of my current feelings. *They* were not being influenced by my pain, *I* was! In order to take back the power over my own life I needed to deal with the past.

To help me move on in my life I did several practical things. I wrote down a record of past injustices and I burnt that record. The ash from those memories sat in the bottom of a metal mixing bowl and, although I still felt the pain, I could tell myself that the events that caused it had now gone; they no longer could have power over me. After a week of checking in on that ash, to make sure the record of those events did not rise again, I scattered that ash in my garden. I watched the wind play with it for a while, but after a couple of days I could no longer see the ash in the garden, it had gone. Whenever I am tempted to recall the injustices of my past and think negatively upon it I remind myself that they are just ash and, as such, have no substance or place in my current life, except to act as fertilizer in assisting my growth and development today.

I don't write these words glibly, I know that some awful things happen to people and such things can scar us for the rest of our lives. However, we can have battle wounds and scars that add to the character of who we are, or we can have festering open sores that stink and rot our flesh. The first one says: 'I'm an old soldier who has won the victory in many battles'; the second one says: 'I lost the battle and my life is in decay.' On this matter we can choose. What will it be for you?

How to build for the future

Rebuilding our lives and our relationships after past negative experiences takes time. Recently I visited a bird park (one of my favourite places) and a beautiful parrot effortlessly removed one of a pair of treasured earrings from my left ear. I didn't notice the bird doing this. I didn't feel a thing! It was later when I noticed the earring had gone that I realized what had happened. I had been warned on entering the bird enclosure that the birds might go for earrings and other jewellery, but somehow I still didn't expect this to happen.

For a while I felt really sad, and even began to dislike the parrot. I tried to reason with myself – 'It was just a parrot doing what birds did; it pecked at something that looked interesting.' 'My earring probably looked like food to this bird; there was no malice intended.' I thought for ages about this event and even wondered what significance it held over my life; what was this event trying to tell me? I concluded that there was no 'higher understanding' at work here, it was just unfortunate. I missed my earrings and pondered on what I could do about it. After a couple of days of phoning the bird park to be told it had not been found, I decided to accept that it was lost. Then I bought some new earrings and put them in my ears. This was a nice thing to do, choosing new earrings and so on, but I still felt sad. As I looked at my

remaining earring, given to me as part of a set after my first gradua-
tion, a thought came to me: 'I've still got one, I could wear it if I had
another hole in my ear.' So, that is what I did. I went to the chemist,
who pierced another hole into my ear so I would be able to wear my
remaining earring; I hadn't lost something after all, I'd gained something! I'm telling you this story as a way of illustrating how good
things can be born from disappointment. Sometimes things are what
we make them.

Wendy at the bird park

For a long time I lived with feelings of disempowerment. I seemed
fated to a future of broken relationships, unemployment, poverty, ill
health and misfortune. I believed that nothing good could ever
happen to me. I lived with chronic depression. It was a long haul
lifting myself out of this muddy quicksand lifestyle that seemed bent
upon dragging me down. I couldn't have done it alone. Although my
faith has sustained me through many a gloomy and stormy experience, it was the assistance of other people and their intervention in
my life that helped to drag me free. Having one other person believe
in us, one other person walk with us through the turmoil of everyday
life, can make the difference between life and death. Two are better
than one in such circumstances. Sometimes it's our families that
support us, sometimes our friends, and sometimes a mixture of both.
We are not meant to live life independently but are created for

interdependence. A single thread may not be strong enough to hold much on its own, but woven in with many others it can support the anchor that holds even the largest ship!

Sharing with others

Although it's good to share our lives with others, there are some things that we need to do alone. If we are to maintain healthy, strong relationships and our safe place within them, we need to keep our sense of self. 'There is only so much of "me" to go around,' I remember thinking. The children want me, my partner wants me, the dog wants me; and then there are all those other daily demands of living. Finding and keeping a balance between relationships, work, leisure, rest and study takes its toll upon anyone. If I have my fingers in too many pies, I'm not going to enjoy any of them.

This is typical for Wendy. I'm always on the go, needing to be here, there and everywhere! I can't sit still for long and I'm not good at doing nothing. Even when I'm focused on one thing, my mind is already racing onto the next. I have constantly to know what will come next, when it will happen and what it all means! I appreciate that this can be overwhelming for other people. My friends have two choices here, they can try to change who I am or they can work with me.

For years I found myself in relationships where others tried to change who I was; their actions only served to sell me the message that I was a dud and, as such, was a hopeless case. If you are experiencing a sense of detachment, a feeling of being overstretched, and your life feels as if it's coming apart at the seams, then maybe you are taking on too much or you are being pulled in too many different directions. We need to sort out our priorities and just what we want for ourselves first; then we can explore how it all fits together. Understanding and accepting that we are different people and that we operate in different ways will assist us in this process. I need to be on the move doing lots of things, this is how I am designed. What about you? Maybe you need to slow down and do less? Maybe you have too many people telling you what to do and you need to stand up for yourself? Only you know what you are comfortable with, and only you can make the choice that fits best with you.

Sharing our lives with another and being in a committed relationship takes two to put in 100 per cent. Having said this we both need to maintain our safe place as individuals and doing this requires that we know ourselves well and our partners too. It's only as we know ourselves that we can share this knowledge with our partner. It takes time to figure out who we are and time to share who we are with another. Giving ourselves this time is crucial. One of the best discoveries I am currently making and comprehending is based upon this understanding. Time together with our partners and daring to share who we each are is essential for maintaining our safe place together.

Time

It seemed to me that we were meant to meet,
How else could you explain it?
So many times I'd walked that street,
So many times sat on that seat.

I know the pain of being alone,
I know the times of isolation.
You came into this time, my home,
You came and broke my desolation.

What was it that drew you to my time?
What was it that you saw?
For me you just looked so fine,
Sitting there that golden Fall.
I noticed you, you noticed me,
We smiled and exchanged glances.
We shared some moments of our time,
Together we took our chances.

It's always risky sharing one's life with another person. None of us knows what the future holds, and taking the time to discover it can be costly. It costs us in a variety of ways: there are emotional costs as well as the financial costs. Is it worth it? I guess each of us must decide for ourselves. I only know that taking the time to explore who I am as a person and being willing to take the time to discover the love of another has been a journey that hasn't been easy but one where the rewards have outweighed the discomforts. I can recommend such a journey to you. As long as you are aware of what the costs will be, you can plan for them. You might find yourself a little short on resources at times, and you might have to dig a bit deeper than usual, but hey, it's all part of the discovery.

CHAPTER 9

Accepting and Celebrating Who I Am

Misdiagnosis and confusion

Throughout my growing years, my scattiness, lack of understanding of others, inability to organize myself, and my difficulties with people were attributed to learning difficulties and schizophrenia. Although I recognize and accept that I have learning difficulties, I believe that the diagnosis of schizophrenia was mistaken.

I didn't do well at school and most of my academic learning occurred after leaving school. As a child I was obsessed with certain other people, animals, and anything that accompanied these interests. I explored medical books and related topics as well as books on dogs, insects and birds. I expected that other people would see everything the same way that I did and I believed they should!

I received my current diagnosis of ASD, specifically Asperger's syndrome, as an adult. Before that time I lived with a lot of confusion, fear and insecurity. Initially I saw other people around me as difficult and very different to myself. For a very long time I was actually waiting for them to realize this and 'fix' themselves. It was only during my teens that I began to realize there were more people like them than there were of those like me. I concluded that I was the one who was different. However, insight into this understanding only added to my frustration because I couldn't change it. At the age of 17 I made my first attempt at suicide.

My over-attachment problems with friends at school and at church meant that others were quickly wary of me or used me to their own ends. I did not recognize the signs that might have alerted me to the 'abusive potential' of some individuals, nor could I separate out the probability of a likely 'good' person to relate to. My gullibility was apparent to all, and this made me very vulnerable. I am hopeful that this book will enable others to escape the kind of trauma I have experienced.

Teenage years are difficult for most of us. No one likes to feel 'different' if it means a sense of isolation and confusion. It's during these years that our bodies change from that of a child to the developing adult. However, unlike typical youths, I didn't notice the underarm hair growth or my breasts enlarging. Getting my first period at the age of ten was a huge shock. I thought I was going to bleed to death! I didn't understand why the other girls at school giggled when the boys passed by or why they wanted to go around in groups. I think this story might be common amongst other youngsters with ASD. Due to our being monotropic it seems to take us a lot longer to connect with things both inside our bodies and outside of them. I don't ever remember having a 'crush' on a boy or wanting them to notice me. I did prefer the company of boys to girls, mainly because they played more interesting games. In the company of girls I often felt uncomfortable and awkward.

However, in spite of not feeling attracted sexually to males at any point in my life, at the age of 20 I married a guy who seemed kind, thoughtful and had a wonderful Matchless 500cc motorbike! We stayed married for almost 20 years, had 4 children, moved countries and learnt a lot of stuff. For the first two years of married life I left home often, to go on journeys. I would leave a note saying, 'Gone away, be back soon.' I certainly didn't recognize that now I was married, my life needed to include my husband and it wasn't the best thing to make decisions without consulting him.

During my married life I had very strong attachments to several other women and experienced obsessive attachment that caused me lots of panic, turmoil and distress. These obsessive attachments dominated my life and I could think of little else outside of these relationships. The idea that I might be gay did not register with me until I was 30 years old.

My husband certainly suffered heaps, as so often one partner does when they are in a partnership with a person who is confused about their identity. I tried to please him and do the right things, but my heart wasn't in the relationship and my husband found it all too much. Eventually he left and set up his own home. As I write this paragraph, he appears to be happily involved with a woman who meets his needs more than I could.

Accepting who I am on both counts (gay and autistic) has been a very difficult process. Many of the individuals in my life abandoned me as I shared my new discoveries with them. I would like to think that people are basically welcoming of others, but it is my experience that this only occurs when an individual does not feel threatened by another. For some reason which I find hard to fathom, many individuals are uncomfortable and do feel threatened by the gay community. However, the evidence is that gay men and women are no more likely to be abusive or offensive than their 'straight' counterparts. In fact, most indecent assaults are committed by heterosexuals; the same is true for child abuse and violence (AIHW 2003).

Coming out

Initial disclosure

Disclosing who we are to others has a number of benefits and pitfalls. For me it was a relief to be given a label that made sense to me. The label enabled me to explore more fully those things that I was experiencing (ASD and homosexuality). However, it also highlighted the depressing realization that Asperger's syndrome was a lifelong disability and being autistic and gay was not going to make building and maintaining relationships very easy.

I didn't choose to be autistic and I didn't choose to be gay, they chose me! There was no way out of this. I remember saying to a person at church, 'How easy would it be for you to give up being heterosexual and become gay?' They laughed at me. At first, whenever I disclosed that I was gay, my friends didn't take me seriously. They said that I was insecure about things and needed lots of 'mothering'. Why was it so difficult to get other people to believe me? Why was it so difficult to be taken seriously and have someone acknowledge my experience? Was it because of my immaturity? Was it because I was a 'late developer' and, at that time, had not been sexually involved with women? Was it because I had married? I guess I'll never really know.

Maybe all of those are factors and maybe those individuals around me just had difficulty seeing that I was a sexual being too.

Whatever the reasons, it was increasingly evident to me that I was not attracted to men, never had been and didn't want to be. I was attracted to the female form though, and always had been. This reality was beginning to filter though my emotions and into the physical responses of my body. One of the things that I notice is that emotionally I seem to take longer than most typical individuals actually to recognize, define and be in a position to utilize many of my emotional states. It's also true to say that I experience one of two states: I am usually highly motivated and connected or pretty much detached. I live with the state of 'non-feeling' more often than the state of feeling, with intense, but short, bursts of emotion in between. These 'bursts' will be connected to my interests and motivated by the same. If that interest happens to be 'a woman' then that is where all of my attention goes.

Having said that I am often detached from much of what goes on around me, I have always been a person with strong sexual desire. But for all of my adolescent years, and some of my early adult life, this was unconnected to any other person. Although I experienced much sexual abuse as a child, I felt unconnected to my own sexuality. I did not fantasize about sex with another person and didn't like to notice intimacy amongst others. Seeing other people physically close, hugging one another or kissing, caused me discomfort. I avoided such behaviour however it was being expressed (written, film or in person). As the years went by and I embarked upon my own gay relationship I longed to be able to be open with my love and affection, even in public places. But, due to the responses of others, showing affection to my partner tends to be confined to the privacy of our own home. At times I feel angry with other people. Why is it OK for them to express their love publicly but not OK for me?

Family life, relationships and friends
I grew up with the belief that family life and relationships in general should all be like those I had encountered through the television shows that I watched. I watched *Little House on the Prairie, The Waltons,*

and children's shows like *Lassie, Champion the Wonder Horse, The Lone Ranger* and *The Famous Five*. In these programmes the essential ingredients to the success of the show were that the good guys always won, people loved and cared for one another, people were interested in each other's worlds, and nothing really bad ever happened to the good guys! When I tried to form relationships with other people, however, they rarely seemed to echo the belief system that I had formed. Some of the individuals I considered to be my 'friends' were often unfriendly, unavailable and full of expectation that I should conform to their ideology. When I failed or didn't manage to live up to expectation, those individuals simply removed their friendship.

Initially, coming to terms with my sexual identity instead of denying it caused me huge discomfort and left me doubled up with pain. It felt like a massive burden had been dropped onto my shoulders and it was unbearable. Then, as I began to find others who had experienced, or were experiencing, the same thing, I found comradeship, fellowship and peace of mind. One of the beautiful rewards of accepting my ASD and my sexuality is that I now only relate to those of like mind. I no longer deliberately expose myself to those who might abuse or trample who I am underfoot.

Being forced to admit that I couldn't stay married was difficult, but it was also a huge relief. I needed to own up to this, not because I wanted to hurt anyone, but because I couldn't live a lie. Telling the folk at my church (where I was an associate pastor), and telling my family and my friends, were very difficult tasks. But this was an essential part of my journey and placed me well on my way to becoming the more confident person that I am today.

The moment of truth

Telling my family that I was autistic didn't seem difficult to me. I thought that they would welcome the diagnosis and realize, as I had done, that it made sense. I expected that everyone would feel the same way that I did. This was a mistake. For the most part my children (then 12, 14, 18 and 20) seemed really interested and happy for me. My youngest son was also being assessed, and in lots of ways, although we were very different people, we were also quite similar. Tim received his diagnosis of Asperger's at a similar time and, along with an assessment of ADHD, he was finally able to access the kind of support he needed at school. The children's father (we were separated at this time) dismissed the diagnoses and said that we were just looking for a way out of our responsibilities. My mother, who had admitted to a close friend that 'Wendy was never normal', outwardly denied that any of her children had difficulties. She seemed uncomfortable with me, and even though I became a successful university graduate, I didn't seem able to please her. The truth is that quite often other people will find both our ASD and our sexuality quite difficult to cope with. Realizing this and accepting this is part of our journey towards self-acceptance. I say this because it's foolishness to believe that our sense of value will come from being valued by others. In reality, we are valuable just because we are! This is intrinsic to the state of being human.

Medication – A help and a hindrance

When I finally got my diagnosis of ASD I was so sure that the treating psychiatrist would say I could stop my neuroleptic medication (seeing as how I was not psychotic and didn't have schizophrenia). This was my first disappointment. The psychiatrist thought that the medication (which I had been taking on and off for more than 25 years) should continue – 'After all it is probably helpful.' I sought the support of the ASD association in my area and they said that such medications were helpful for lots of individuals but that I should talk this over with my doctor and aim at reducing it, to see how I went.

Eventually the psychiatrist agreed to this idea. It took another five years before the doctor finally said that I could cease taking the medication altogether. This was done abruptly and without any consultation with me about possible side-effects! With the antipsychotic medication withdrawal came a lack of motivation, seemingly endless tummy-upsets and increased difficulty with concentration. At times I thought I was mad! My doctor prescribed an antidepressant called Zoloft. No one explored the possibility that my experiences were probably connected to fast withdrawal from neuroleptic medication. I took Zoloft for 12 months, but with each day of taking it I felt nauseated and had a strange icy feeling around the inside of my head. I was relieved to stop this medication, even though it probably took the edge off my anxieties and helped me cope with my daily life.

It is not unusual for us as individuals with ASD to need medication. I just want to echo though that medication will not solve all of our issues. In fact, at times it might make things worse. Some medications will negatively affect our libido and this can cause problems in our relationships. Some cause our metabolism to slow and we might become more prone to putting on weight. There could be a number of side-effects with any medications we take, so it's always a good idea to check this out with a doctor whom you trust.

Finding myself in education

Returning to school

I left school as a 15-year-old. I hadn't done very well at school and it seemed that an academic career was out of the question for me. Instead I went away from home to do a pre-nursing course at college. I actually did quite well in my course, but the practical side of things was difficult. I wasn't successful with my attempts at being employed, but I did long for more independence. When my youngest son was eight, I returned to school. I wanted to go to university and this was one of the prerequisites. I did well as a nearing 40-year-old amongst 17- to 18-year-olds. I found the group of students I was part of to be accepting and supportive. I spoke freely to them of my difficulties with academic study. They helped me with putting my essays onto the computer, and also with developing and structuring my ideas. The teacher for Australian history was interested in me because of my choice of topic for my project. Instead of the usual range of historical study I chose 'Women in the 1930s and cross-dressing'. Although I was not fully 'out' to my friends at this time, I found my studies enriched my understanding and helped me to appreciate the battles of other women in earlier years who had struggled to exist in a world dominated by men.

University – A new experience

I got a place at Monash University in Victoria to study social work. It was during my first year at university that I fully accepted I was gay. My divorce came through and my new partner and I seriously decided to set up home together. We had been soulmates for more than ten years, and our relationship was sound. I knew we had to tell the children that their mum was now going to live as a lesbian, not just in name but also in actuality, with another woman. This woman was like an aunt to them, and they loved her. For the first time the children began to understand the reality of their situation. What would their friends say? How could they bring friends home and have them realize their mother was gay? What did it all mean? They were furious with me. 'How dare you do this to us, Mum,' my daughter said. I tried to explain that I was not doing it to anyone... She didn't understand, and because I wouldn't change my mind she left home. My eldest son also left home. My daughter went to live with a lady from church; my son went to live with his father. The impact of this on me was devastating. I had thought that my children would see that this was good for us all. I failed to appreciate that they were embarrassed by me and, in their still childlike way, believed that I should put them first above any other. I had no income (only an education allowance), two of my children had left home, and I felt completely isolated.

When I tried to talk to friends, they were astounded. 'How can a reasonable and intelligent person like you be doing this?' they said. 'Men were designed to relate sexually with women. Not women with women,' said a close friend. 'I mean, only a man has the right append-age for the job.' I failed to see what 'the right appendage' had to do with a loving relationship where one could be honest and at home with oneself. A meeting was called at church and the committee asked me to resign. I complied. From that day to this most of the 'friends' I thought I had removed themselves from our friendship. I still feel sad about this today.

At university I found a very different culture. At uni I experienced respect and support. In particular my academic work was respected. I still had lots of difficulties with social events and avoided them, but my desire to learn was welcomed by the lecturers. I found other students who were gay and would involve myself in debates about religion and homosexuality. I obtained an assessment for my academic difficulties with reading, writing and maths. As well as being an Asperger's person I was diagnosed as being dyslexic, matholexic (my word for difficulties with maths) and, much later in my career, I discovered I had attention deficit hyperactivity disorder (ADHD). The university made provision for my difficulties. They were never seen as a problem!

The university was happy to use my abundant energy and enthusiasm. Instead of constantly being told to 'Sit still, Wendy', it was 'What do you think you might like to do to contribute to uni life?' No one had ever asked me what I wanted; most of my life I had been told what to do by others who knew what was best for me. It is true, had I been asked, I might have said that I wanted to become an artist, a writer or a missionary in some distant place. My dreams might have seemed a bit out of reach at some points in my life, but this is not a good reason to stamp on them!

As a keen writer and researcher, I was offered the role of editor for the university newspaper. I was so excited! This was the first time in my life I had ever been offered a job of this nature. In the past I had been considered with some contempt as 'not being able to do anything'. As a child at school, for example, when it came to other students choosing the members they wanted for their team, Wendy was never chosen, and teacher had to intervene to put her into a team. I was not good at appreciating the 'social complexities' of human relating and it was easier to walk around the playground following the white line than join in with some children's games that made no sense to me and failed to engage any of my interests. The only games I was welcome in were those where other children found fun in teasing or bullying me.

Acceptance

When I received my diagnosis of ASD I went to the Disability Liaison Officer at uni and gave them my written report. Again I was very fortunate, I had a person who was willing to listen. 'Wendy, what difficulties do you experience?' she asked me. Initially it was hard to locate 'difficulties' because the question came without a framework for answering it, but with a bit of prompting I was able to respond. I said that it was very difficult to listen to a lecture and take notes at the same time. I explained that I wasn't good at doing two things at once. 'Oh, that's easy,' she said. 'We'll get you a note taker.' I also told her how I got lost easily and didn't cope with finding my way around or with lots of noise, lights and people. She assigned me to a 'peer support' person who showed me around campus and waited to assist me in locating places. I also was allowed to take exams in a separate room to other students, given extra reading time and was allowed to check in with the invigilator that I had understood questions. Accommodating needs like these, so that all students can have equal opportunity, should be the normal procedure for any institution of learning.

I was also glad that I had disclosed my sexuality to my fellow students and I was fortunate to have a positive response. I know that not all of my friends found this true for their situation. I wonder if it was easier for some to accept my sexuality because I was a woman. How would it have been if I were a man?

Outcomes

Confidence and family relationships

When we grow up in our families we come to expect that our parents and family life will always be the way it has always been. We don't expect it to change much, and if it does we have strong views as to what those changes might include. Dramatic changes with regard to one's usual role and one's sexuality are not expected, and most other family members will experience some discomfort with these changes. My children were finding it very difficult to accommodate their Mum's new lifestyle. Not only was Mum home less often, she had a really keen interest in understanding homosexuality and the world of disability, especially ASD. In the past they had been used to Mum's obsessive disposition towards insects, birds, animals and Christianity. In fact being a Christian had been Mum's preoccupation ever since they could remember. Suddenly, Mum was not attending church any more; no more bible study groups; no more prayer meetings. I missed my church involvement, and letting it all go was a big change for me. It took years to come to terms with the issue that even though my Christian faith hadn't changed, due to my gay lifestyle I was not welcome in most churches. My children were quite worried that their Mum had lost her mind. I don't know if they stayed away from our home because of their need to remain in a more familiar environment or if they just couldn't fathom what else to do.

During the first couple of years after my divorce I experienced waves of a very uncomfortable feeling. It would just 'whoosh' up from inside my tummy and I couldn't eat or sleep. I felt like I had failed my children, failed my husband and failed my heavenly Father. 'What kind of a Christian does this to her family?' I asked myself. The truth, as I saw it, was that I had to be honest. Somehow I believed that my heavenly Father loved and understood me. If anyone accepted me for who I was, He did! I took comfort in this belief and in my studies.

My mother made it very plain to me that she didn't accept my sexuality, my chosen partner or my lifestyle. Whenever I shared with her some of my academic success she seemed pleased to have me as a daughter. Whenever my ASD presented me with a problem, however, she became cross and removed herself from me. I so often felt abandoned and despairing. Fortunately for me, my few remaining friends stayed loyal and supportive.

Career opportunities

I continued to do well in my studies and began to envisage a career in the behavioural sciences. I started a support group for parents of children with ASD. The parents said that my talking of my experiences helped them to understand their children better. They suggested that I write about my experiences and even consider a career as a teacher. 'Wow, what a concept!' I remember thinking. 'Who would have ever thought that Wendy, diagnosed as being intellectually disabled, as having ASD and learning difficulties, would be thought of as an individual with skills useful to others!' I was ecstatic! The issue here is that actually many of us with ASD are very able indeed. We are loyal, trustworthy, committed to our areas of interest and, in fact, we might be your best asset!

I had always found 'written expression' a great medium for arranging my thoughts and reviewing an understanding. I spent a couple of years putting a manuscript together as an autobiography, then set about finding a publisher. At the same time I travelled overseas to continue with my social work studies, as an exchange student. During five months spent at the University of Bradford in the UK, I concentrated upon my studies from Monash by distance education, managed the compulsory studies at Bradford and pursued my writing. I eventually found a publisher and gained a literary agent. Sheila, my agent, encouraged me to keep writing. After my second book was published (I self-published my first book, a book of poetry) Sheila told me that it would be the first of many. To have such 'faith' in my work, my ability and me was totally foreign to me. I cried a lot at that time.

Disclosing critical aspects of my life experience in my book *Life Behind Glass* was quite painful for me. Revisiting my growing up, my schooling, my teenage experiences, getting married and then becoming a divorcee, all opened up wounds that I had wanted to forget. However, maybe my life today needed me to revisit my life then. Maybe I am wiser and stronger for having faced those times. It seems to me that writing and then reading what I write helps me to cement my understanding. My experiences take on meaning; they get connected to reality and I am even more able to make sense of things. I know that my learning is delayed and I seem to be slower than many others at adjusting to understanding, either of self or of others. The great thing about this understanding though is once it jells it really sticks!

Disclose or not?

It has been a gradual process of writing, getting my work published and completing the various studies that I have undertaken at different universities. I love to study, research my material and write about it. At times I have been so excited about a topic that it has been hard to contain it. I talk incessantly to others and have got myself into trouble because they are not interested. For example, when I told other students that I got an A grade I expected them to rejoice with me. It was only later that one friend explained to me that I came across as 'bragging'. My talking about my high grades to others with lower grades made them feel uncomfortable. In fact some students were even cross with me! I've been known to talk on and on and on about the things that interest me. This failure to pick up on, or be sensitive to, the fact that another person might not share my interest has taken me years to realize. Disclosure is one aspect of 'telling', but I am learning that there is a time to disclose and a time to refrain from disclosure.

Academically I still wrestle with what aspects of my knowledge I should or should not share. Learning to be honest, whilst being discreet and sensitive to others, is not my forte!

I am aware that once I have spoken I cannot take the words back. However, what I fail to recognize are which situations I should share with another, who that 'other' should be and when I should share. For me, when something is on my mind it completely takes over my thoughts, and there is no space for anything else. Thus, it will be those thoughts that get expressed, even at times when it is not appropriate to tell the person those thoughts. I know this after the event because the person might say, 'I don't need to know that Wendy.' Sometimes the person will become 'different'. I can tell that something has changed for that person, but I might not be able to define what that change is, nor what the implications of that change might be. I've had a measure of success, though, when I've checked in with the other person and asked them if I can tell them what's going on for me. At times I've had to accept that my timing might not be good or that I need to wait for a better time to talk about things. I think many of us, as individuals with ASD, find delayed gratification quite difficult. I know it's something that I need to practise!

It is only this year (I am now 52 years old) that I realized it is OK not to disclose all my thoughts and feelings to my partner. I believed that a partnership meant 'sharing' every aspect of myself with the other. When I discovered that it was OK to have thoughts, ideas, dreams and interests that were one's own and didn't automatically need to be shared, I was intrigued. I still felt some discomfort with this realization, but I also felt some relief. It was a relief to know that if I chose not to disclose my thoughts, it was OK. I have come to understand that I am not lying if I choose to keep some information to myself. In fact, at times, other individuals are not interested in what's happening for me and they prefer it if I just take time to listen to them.

When I chose actively to engage in the gay lifestyle, I found it much easier being 'out' when I was amongst others who were like me. This has been true also for my ASD. I find that being with other individuals on the spectrum gives me a freedom to be myself. I don't need to struggle to hide my emotions or to wear myself thin trying to perform so as not to upset someone.

Acceptance and emotional growth

'No pain no gain' a friend states. How I wish this were not true, but I think it probably is right. I know I have felt the joy of satisfaction from eating after I have experienced hunger. I know the relief I have experienced once I realized my anxiety was unfounded. Then there is the ecstasy of discovering a good grade written on the Results Board in the hall at the university. If I hadn't first felt the hunger, the anxiety, the discomfort of waiting, I could not have known the relief! This is also my experience with disclosure. There have been moments of utter despair; times of sheer agony, heartache and helplessness. I have experienced huge disappointment, frustration and physical torment. Today, I can look back over those episodes not with gladness that they happened but with some comprehension and appreciation of the outcomes they have brought for my life.

How will we ever educate others or assist them in their understanding if we don't disclose to them? We need to start by acknowledging 'self' to ourselves; then we can begin to acknowledge 'self' to others. Accepting who I am, warts and all, is the best gift I can give to myself and to others. Self-confidence can only reign well in a culture of self-acceptance.

This depends upon me, not upon the value I receive from others. Obviously, my self-confidence is endorsed and enhanced by the positive actions of others, but it cannot begin there. The responsibility of my accepting 'me' is mine to begin with. This is the foundation for my current and future life. I know that some would argue that self-confidence begins with having others believe in us first, then we can believe in ourselves. Maybe it's that old question of what comes first, the chicken or the egg? I don't know the answer. I only know that I need to believe in me. If I wait for others to promote my abilities and take no action until they do, then I could be waiting a very long time and I might be missing the moment, hence the opportunity might be lost.

Being me, relationships and real friends

In my experience people are sometimes uncomfortable around me. It would seem that my very presence 'exposes' them in some way or another. Maybe my behaviour causes them to feel embarrassed or maybe they just don't feel that comfortable with themselves, and this is more evident when they are with me. This seems to have been the situation with some of my friends in the past. For me, coming to terms with this understanding has been very difficult. I know that the aspects about myself that are not pleasing to others seem to be the things that I cannot change. This means that by disclosing who I am (gay and autistic) I am exposing any potential relationship to the risk of not developing. It is, therefore, tempting to conform to expectation and not upset the delicate balance of human need and demand. I'm just not good at this! I have tried to be 'the wife', the good Christian woman, the mother. I actually think I did a good job, while it lasted. The crunch came when I could no longer live a lie. It was OK for a while because I didn't have the right name for who I was. I conformed to the label I'd been landed with, even though it was very uncomfortable. But, once reality set in and I knew the truth, I could no longer hide behind the make-believe set-up I'd grown up in and adopted as 'my life'.

'You shall know the truth and the truth shall set you free.' This quote from scripture holds true for me and I am glad. I'm not glad that others are embarrassed by the 'truth' that is Wendy. I'm not glad that some are disappointed and saddened by this truth. However, these are their difficulties, not mine. Their problems with who I am are for them to solve and sort out. I know that my real friends are bigger and stronger than the discomforts they feel with any of 'Wendy's Wendyness'…they are committed to my well-being and to our mutual friendship. At times my own disclosures of difficulty and doubt set others free to share their difficulties too. If we only share our achievements and successes, I think we set the standard too high and others may feel as if they cannot be themselves. It's as if being who they are means accepting and disclosing to themselves that they are imperfect beings. Surely we all need to know that this is true for each of us, and it's OK?

Knowledge, self and the future

In this chapter I have disclosed much about my being autistic, gay and 'happy' with who I am. This has required courage and honesty from me. I hope it has been useful to you. I hope that you will join the community of 'accepting others'; the embers in the fireplace will burn longer and brighter when surrounded by others burning with them. None of us need be in this battle alone. There is some evidence to suggest that the incidence of homosexuality is higher amongst individuals on the autistic spectrum than in the typical population. There is evidence to show that the population of people with ASD is growing. If we want to be involved with the building of a better future for our children and for the human race in general, then we need to be involved with disclosure. No longer can we afford to sit on the fence and let others do the jumping. We need to be jumping with them. Self-confidence can develop as one 'bites the bullet', takes the plunge, dives in and learns to swim. If we are going to make a difference to the world we all live in then we need to stand together, with our heads raised to the sun. Being autistic, gay and building successful relationships will take courage, commitment and compassion. Building and maintaining any relationship is for the brave. Let's be in it, if we can, for the long haul.

This book has been a journey for some of us and not always an easy one. Most journeys we embark upon work better when we prepare for them. Relationships are a bit like journeys. They involve travelling through life with others. When we know ourselves, can accept who we are and are willing to work on our personal growth, then our chances of successful relationships are higher than if we bury our heads in the sand and blame the rest of the world for when things go wrong. Preparing for a journey might involve having plans, provisions and personal expectations. There is nothing wrong with these. But plans may change; provisions may dwindle and personal expectations may meet with disappointment. What will we do then? I reckon we might need to have a back-up plan. Being as prepared as we can will double our chances. Life might deliver sunshine, rain, storms or rainbows. Knowing this is half the battle, preparing for it gives us the winning edge.

APPENDIX 1

Couple Activities Just for Fun

Have you ever considered doing things together that are fun but require a team effort? There's tandem riding, kayaking, walking, yoga and lots more. Or perhaps you would like something less strenuous? How about stamp collecting, bird watching or designing a vege patch?

'I like dancing with my partner. Even if we are on our own at home, it just lightens things up a bit and gives us the opportunity to let our hair down together.'

'For me watching videos does it really. Sometimes we have a whole evening of watching our favourite videos. We get in the pop-corn and the choc ices, sit back and enjoy ourselves.'

'At times we decide to swap recipes and Jane cooks the dessert whilst I take on the role of main course provider. That way I get to choose the wine!'

Maybe you can explore your fun activities together and make this a regular event?

I love crossword puzzles and word searches. I have compiled one of each for you to share together. They might not be difficult to do, but perhaps you can use them as a conversation piece. You will notice that the words in these activities are all connected to relationships in one way or another. I hope that you will find them useful. Maybe they will act as a trigger for further discussion. Maybe they will start you thinking about how they might apply to you and to your relationships. I hope you enjoy them.

My partner does not like games with words very much and prefers to play cards. So we play the games she chooses at times and at other times we go with my choice. I have found that playing chess (which I find really difficult) is a helpful game for me because my partner likes to play chess and because it appears to be a good strategy for supporting my poor memory and concentration skills (it aids both).

Other games you can share together are things like making up lists of words for the letters of the alphabet. You might find if you stipulate a theme for this game it can become quite interesting! For example, 'How many animals can you name beginning with the letter J?' Or, 'How many items of interest to women can you name beginning with the letter P?' It might be interesting to note the things you think are of interest to women and the things your partner thinks of as interesting.

I'm sure if you think about it you could come up with other ideas for fun activities that you can share together, whether they are inside activities or outside ones. There really is a large world of discovery about one another that is waiting for you!

Relationships crossword

Below are some fun activities that you can share together. I love words and words are a great way to explore one's thoughts and feelings. You will notice that words in the activity sheets are all connected to relationships in one way or another. I hope that you will find them useful. Maybe they will act as a trigger for further discussion, or maybe they will start you thinking about how they might apply to you and your relationships. I hope you enjoy them.

Down
1. Two is company
2. My first choice (of television programme, colour, etc.)
3. A good way to communicate
4. Smaller individuals
5. I feel ... threatened

Across
1. Not to be done lightly
6. I get too ... at times
7. Using in common with another
8. Let me know; get in touch
9. This is what turns me on
10. Seeing red
11. I'm not good at this; making eye contact
12. Fun times together
13. Red is my favourite

Relationships wordsearch

Find each of the following words.

ADVENTURE	DINNER	IMPORTANT	RISKY
APARTMENT	DRIVE	KITCHEN	ROLES
BABIES	ENTERTAINMENT	LEAVE	SAD
BEDROOM	EMAIL	ORIENTATION	SAME
BIKE	ENERGY	OUT	SEPARATE
BUS	FAMILY	PETS	SOFTLY
CASUAL	HAPPINESS	RADIO	SLOW
CHALLENGE	HEALTH	READING	SMOOTH
CHAT	HOME	READY	TOGETHER
CHORES	HOLIDAYS	REGULAR	USEFUL
DIFFERENT	ILL	RESTLESS	WORK

```
E O R I S K Y U S E F U L R E G U L A R I L O
V S T E N T E R T A I N M E N T C A S U A L P
I Y N G M A L H S T E O A D V E N T U R E D M
R A H A P P I N E S S I K I T C H E N D G I R
D D U T T T S D D A E T S A M E D T G A N N N
Y I A B N E E O A S L A H H E E M A S S E N Y
E L I T I A I U M E P T A O C H O R E S L E P
K O I B O D T O S E S N H M R R O A L I L R R
I H A M A G O R T B E E N E H R R P O S A E D
B B S R A T E S O U T I C H A T D E R O H S T
L A D T H F T T Y P E R S I S M E S S F C T E
I C E W O R K S H D M O A U A D B S Y T A L K
A R I T L E A V E E A I B S S L O W I L L E S
M D I F F E R E N T R E E N E R G Y B Y A S K
E T A A P A R T M E N T R G R E A D I N G S G
I R R A E E E A I D L R T R H H N L E R T N I
```

Solution to crossword

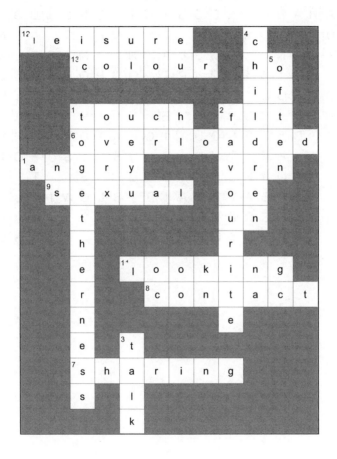

Solution to Wordsearch

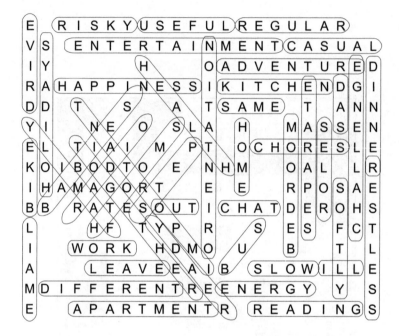

Worksheets

The following worksheets aim to increase understanding of the autism spectrum. You and your partner might find them useful as a means of exploring your understanding of ASDs and checking with each other whether your understanding and/or experiences are similar. If they are different, you might like to consider what this means for you both and how you might accommodate your differences.

WORKSHEET 1

The autism continuum – How does it express itself?

Classic autism

Asperger's syndrome

PDD-NOS (Pervasive Developmental Disorder–Not Otherwise Specified

WORKSHEET 2

COGNITION: 'mental operations such as thinking, conceiving, reasoning, symbolizing, insight, expectancy, complex rule use, imagery, belief, intentionally, problem solving and so forth' (Reber 1995, p.133).

With this definition in mind discuss and record what you consider to be the effects of monotropism on cognition.

For example: If I don't have the same concept of an event as my partner does, how might this impact upon our relationship?

WORKSHEET 3

LANGUAGE: 'conventional symbols through which we convey meaning…the medium through which we code our feelings, thoughts, ideas and experiences' (Reber 1995, p.406).

With this definition in mind discuss and record what you consider to be the effects of monotropism on the social exchanges you have with your partner.

For example: If it takes you longer to process language than it does your partner, do you allow for this in your relationships? If you do, how do you? If you don't how might you change this?

WORKSHEET 4

SOCIALIZATION: 'process whereby an individual acquires the knowledge, values, facility with language, social skills and social sensitivity enabling them to integrate into and behave adaptively within a society' (Reber 1995, p.732).

With this definition in mind discuss and record what you consider to be the effects of monotropism on the social aspects of your relationships.

For example: On a scale of 1–10 with 1 being you are very sensitive to the feelings of others and 10 being you hardly notice the feelings of others, how do you rate your sense of sensitivity to your partner's feelings and their sensitivity to your feelings? Taking into account your answers, how could you work best with what you come up with?

WORKSHEET 5

Trust and Sexuality

Do I feel safe with you?

Do you feel safe with me?

Do we meet our sexual needs?

Ben Roe's Sexual Orientation Worksheet

If you want to explore your own sexual orientation, here is a simple research instrument that was used by Fritz Klein and others. It is a refinement of the Kinsey Scale which ranked behavior and 'psychologic reactions' on a scale from 0 to 6, with 0 being exclusively heterosexual, 6 being exclusively homosexual, and 3 being equally homosexual/heterosexual (Kinsey, Pomeroy and Martin 1948).

Klein wanted to test his idea that sexual orientation was a 'dynamic, multi-variable process,' so he developed the Klein Sexual Orientation Grid. He thought that an individual's sexual orientation was composed of sexual and non-sexual variables which differed over time. There are

- three variables which directly describe the sexual self (attraction, fantasy, and behavior)
- three which describe aspects considered crucial to the composition of sexual orientation (emotional preference, social preference, and heterosexual or homosexual lifestyle)
- and also the variable of self-identification.

This form can be used privately for your own reflection or in a sharing group, or in less personal educational settings. You may make a copy of the Grid with the scales and explanatory text and then fill it out. Following the presentation of the instrument is a series of things to think about or explore in a group.

The following text closely follows that of the Klein article.

Klein Sexual Orientation Grid

Variable	Past	Present	Ideal
A. Sexual Attraction			
B. Sexual Behavior			
C. Sexual Fantasies			
D. Emotional Preference			
E. Social Preference			
F. Self-Identification			
G. Hetero/Gay Lifestyle			

Scale 1

Other sex only	Other sex mostly	Other sex somewhat more	Both sexes equally	Same sex somewhat more	Same sex mostly	Same sex only
1	2	3	4	5	6	7

Scale 2

Hetero only	Hetero mostly	Hetero somewhat more	Hetero/ Gay	Gay somewhat more	Gay mostly	Gay only
1	2	3	4	5	6	7

A. Sexual Attraction

In this grid, you will be choosing three numbers, one for each of three aspects of your life: your past, your present, and your ideal. Beginning with your past (up to a year ago), ask yourself where you fit on this scale and select the number that best describes you. Write this number in the corresponding box marked 'past' on the line for Variable A (Sexual Attraction) on the grid. Then select a number that describes your present sexual attraction using the preceding year as the time period you consider. For a number of people it is the same number; for others it is different. Write this number in the box marked 'present' on the line for Variable A. Now ask yourself which number you would choose to be if it were a matter of choice or will. Remember there are no right or wrong numbers. When you finish writing this last number in the box marked Ideal for Variable A on the grid you should have completed the three boxes for Variable A.

B. Sexual Behavior

Here we look at actual behavior as opposed to sexual attraction. With whom do you have sex? Use the scale to rate yourself. As with the previous scale, choose a number for past, present, and ideal sexual behavior, then enter the numbers on the grid, this time under Variable B.

C. Sexual Fantasies

The third variable is sexual fantasy. Whether they occur during masturbation, while daydreaming, as part of our real lives or purely in our imaginations, fantasies provide insight. Rate yourself on the scale, then enter the numbers on the grid.

D. Emotional Preference

Our emotions directly influence, if not define, the actual physical act of love. Ask yourself if you love and like only the opposite sex or if you are also emotionally close to the same sex. Find out where you fit on the scale; rate yourself as with the other scales. Enter the numbers on the grid.

E. Social Preference

Though closely allied to emotional preference, social preference is often different. You may love only women but spend most of your social life with men. Some people, of all orientations, only socialize with their own sex, while others socialize with the opposite gender exclusively. Where are you on the scale? Choose three numbers as you have on the other scales.

F. Self-Identification

Your sexual self-definition is a strong variable since self-image strongly affects our thoughts and actions. In several cases, a person's present and past self-identification differs markedly from their ideal. Choose three numbers on Scale 2 and fill in the numbers on the grid.

G. Heterosexual/Homosexual Lifestyle

Some heterosexuals only have sex with the opposite sex but prefer to spend the majority of their time with gay people. On the other hand, homosexual or bisexual persons may prefer to live exclusively in the gay world, the heterosexual world, or even to live in both worlds. Lifestyle is the seventh variable of sexual orientation. Where do you tend to spend time and with whom? Choose three numbers on Scale 2 as you have on the other scales and enter them on the grid.

Bobbi Keppel is a social worker who used this grid in educational workshops. She and Alan Hamilton write, 'New concepts and new research offer opportunities to change the way people understand and conceptualize sexual orientation' (Keppel and Hamilton n.d.). They have found that using this type of exercise has helped people 'to ask questions and discuss sexual orientation more easily.' In their paper, they present the grid as a set of scales which form a 3-dimensional stack of cards or block. (She also adds 'Political Identity,' 'Physical Affection Preference,' and 'Community Affiliation' as additional scales, replacing 'Hetero/Gay Lifestyle.')

They write that it is helpful to start with an introduction of the Kinsey Scale as the first opportunity to reconceptualize sexual orientation. This scale was the main influence towards reconceptualization of sexual orientation for many years. Klein, Sepekoff and Wolf's (1985) work offered the opportunity to broaden understanding even further.

The element of time is more explicit in the Klein Grid, and the addition of the Ideal allows consideration of intention and the future. Taking all of the scales or grid locations as a whole gives a picture of one's sexual orientation over time and can be helpful in discussing the concept as well as 'identifying commonalities and differences.'

If you are doing this exercise alone, try to reflect on how your 'constellation' of ratings differs from that of someone you know well, a close friend or partner. If you are in a small study group with a high enough level of trust, those who are comfortable sharing their choices may do so. It will become clear that even those who share the same self-identification differ in their makeup in interesting ways. Similarities will also emerge, not only between those who share self-identifications but between those who identify differently.

Keppel and Hamilton write, 'Sexual identity (how people think of themselves) sometimes has little to do with their sexual behavior. Three different people may have the same distribution of sexual behavior in the past and/or present, but have three different sexual identities: homosexual, bisexual, or heterosexual.' Those who identify as heterosexual may not have the exact same behavior, or those who identify as bisexual may not have the same lifestyle, as another example.

Be observant of how people's identity, behavior, or fantasies may change over time. Research such as Klein's, and the experience of many people shows significant fluidity in self-identification. Keppel and Hamilton observe,

> Many people were sure that they would be, for instance, heterosexual all their lives, but discovered later that they no longer were. It there behooves one to treat others as one would like to be treated, regardless of one's current sexual identity, as one's sexual identity may change.

(One hears an echo of Jesus in this statement.)

As you reflect on any fluidity in your own ratings (or those shared with you), also reflect how your particular self-identification and self-understanding was valid for you at each particular time of your life.

Also note how one's community of support (or lack thereof) can influence one's self-identification or identity. Someone may identify as homosexual or heterosexual, for example, where there is no support for being bisexual. Some may even identify as heterosexual where there is no support for being bisexual or homosexual.

One of the main outcomes of using this grid can be to illustrate that there is not just one sexual orientation: heterosexual; that there are not just two sexual orientations, heterosexual and homosexual; and even that there are not just three sexual orientations, heterosexual, homosexual and bisexual, but indeed a whole range of complex, interacting, and fluid factors in our sexuality.

If you use this grid in a larger group, it may be helpful to have people share in groups of 6 or 8, or perhaps only take the worksheet home to fill out and think about.

A Sensory Profile Discussion Sheet

Our senses are the first place of contact with the world around us. We see, hear, smell, touch and taste as a way of connecting to and understanding what we are experiencing. Sometimes our senses can be very sensitive and this can cause conflict in our relationships. Outlined below are some questions and statements that could prompt discussion between you and your partner. This could be a useful tool in guiding and furthering understanding of each other.

- Which 'sense' do you feel the most at home with? Sight, sound, smell, touch or taste? Perhaps you relate best to more than one sense?

- Does your partner's after-shave or perfume bother you?

- Would you prefer that they didn't use one?

- Where do you like to be touched the most? Are there some areas of your body that you prefer not to be touched?

- Do you like the sound of your partner's voice? Are there times when you would prefer them not to speak?

- Are you comfortable making love with the lights on? Is it easier to make love to your partner when you close your eyes, or do you feel that you need to 'see' in order to know what to do next?

- Do you find that you need lots of touch to stimulate you sexually, or does too much touch close you down?

Our senses are constantly giving us messages. Some of these are welcome but others are not. The difficulty is that because we are each different to the other we may have different sensory needs and thresholds. Understanding this and learning about how we each operate can help to foster successful sexual intimacy between us. If we don't understand how we operate, then the differences between us could build into conflict and eventual resentment.

Check the following statements and see if they apply to you.

- I need you to slow down and take more time with me; kissing me and stroking me help me to relax.

- Because you spend so much time kissing and cuddling me I get overloaded and I switch off from you.

- I can concentrate better with the radio on.

- I can relate more easily to you when you stop talking and allow me to focus.

- I miss the feeling of 'skin'.

- I need to keep my PJs on because I can't cope with the feeling of skin on skin.

- I can feel you better when we don't face each other.

- I can't cope with having you too close to me; lying on our sides back to back gives me the closeness I can cope with.

- I need you to touch me firmly; light touch is uncomfortable for me.

References

AIHW (2003) *Child Protection Australia (2001–02)*. Canberra, Australia: Australian Institute of Health and Welfare.

Asperger, H. (1944) 'Die "Autistischen" im Kindesalter.' *Archiv für Psychiatrie und Nervenkrankheiten 117*, 76–136.

Carol, L. (2003) 'Autism, anxiety and stress related disorders.' Autism Conference, New South Wales, Australia.

Keppel, B. and Hamilton, A. (n.d.) *Using the Klein Scale to Teach about Sexual Orientation*. Brochure published by the Bisexual Resource Center, P.O. Box 639, Cambridge, MA 02140.

Kinsey, A.C., Pomeroy, W.B. and Martin, C.E. (1948) *Sexual Behavior in the Human Male*. Philadelphia, PA: W.B. Saunders.

Klein, F., Sepekoff, B. and Wolf, T.J. (1985) 'Sexual orientation: A Multi-Variable Dynamic Process.' In F. Klein and T.J. Wolf (eds) *Two Lives to Lead: Bisexuality in Men and Women*. New York: Harrington Park Press. (Also published as *Bisexualities: Theory and Research* by Haworth Press, 1985.)

Lawson, W. (2001) *Understanding and Working with the Spectrum of Autism: An Insider's View*. London: Jessica Kingsley Publishers.

Lawson, W. (2003) *Build Your Own Life: A Self-help Guide for Individuals with Asperger Syndrome*. London: Jessica Kingsley Publishers.

Loefler, I. (2004) 'Of evolution and homosexuality'. *British Medical Journal 328*, 7451, 1325.

Mesibov, G.B. (2001) 'Autism and sexuality.' Autism Conference, Sydney, Australia.

Mortlock, J. (1993) *Socio-sexual Development of People with Autism and Related Learning Disabilities*. Based on a presentation given at an Inge Wakehurst Trust study weekend. Available via the National Autistic Society website (www.nas.org.uk).

Moxon, L. (2000) 'Sex education for young adults with autism and Asperger syndrome: The fourth "R" – Relationships.' Presentation at the Inaugural World Autism Conference, Melborne, Australia.

Moxon, L. (2001) 'Developing a policy on sexuality for a provider service for people with Autistic Spectrum Disorder.' In *An Autism Odyssey: Collected Papers from the Durham Conference*. University of Sunderland: Autism Research Unit.

Murray, D.K.C. (1992) 'Attention tunnelling and autism.' In *Living with Autism: The Individual, the Family and the Professional*. Autism Research Unit, University of Sunderland, UK.

Newport, J. and Newport, M. (2002) *Autism – Asperger's and Sexuality: Puberty and Beyond*. Arlington, TX: Future Horizons.

Pukki, H. (2003) 'Developing expressions of sexuality: The perspective and experiences of able autistic people.' *Good Autism Practice (GAP) 4*, 2, 60–61.

Reber, S. (1995) *Dictionary of Psychology* (2nd edition). London: Penguin Books.

Segar, M. (2001) *Coping: A Survival Guide for People with Asperger Syndrome*. Nottingham: Early Years Diagnostic Centre.

Schopler, E. and Mesibov, G.B. (1993) *Autism in Adolescents and Adults*. New York: Plenum.

Further Reading and Resources

AASECT (American Association of Sex Educators, Counselors, and Therapists) call 1-319-895-8407 for the name of a certified sex therapist in your area.

Aston, M. (2003) *Aspergers in Love*. London: Jessica Kingsley Publishers.

Attwood, T. (1999) 'Modifications to cognitive behaviour therapy to accommodate the cognitive profile of people with Asperger's Syndrome.' http://www.tonyattwood.com.au

Attwood, T. and Henault, I. (2002) 'Sexual profile of adults with Asperger's syndrome: The need for understanding, support and education.' Presentation at the Inaugural World Autism Congress, Melbourne, Australia.

Bloom, Y. and Bhargava, D. (2003) *Let's Talk Together Package! Great Ideas Manual Update*. Beecroft: Innovative Communication Programming. http://www.innovativeprogramming.net.au

Bolick, T. (2001) *Asperger Syndrome and Adolescence: Helping Preteens and Teens Get Ready for the Real World*. Gloucester, MA: Fair Winds Press.

Christoff, K.J. and Kane, S.R. (1991) 'Relationship building for students with autism.' *Teaching Exceptional Children 23* (2), 49–51.

Cutting, A. and Dunn, J. (1999) 'Theory of mind, emotion understanding, language and family background: Individual differences and inter-relations.' *Child Development 70* (4), 853–865.

Gray, C. (1994) *Comic Strip Conversations*. Arlington, TX: Future Horizons.

Ford, J.A. and Milosky, L.M. (2003) 'Inferring emotional reactions in social situations: Differences in children with language impairment.' *Journal of Speech, Language and Hearing Research 46* (1), 21-31.

Frith, C. and Frith, U. (2000) 'The physiological basis of theory of mind: Functional neuroimaging studies.' In S. Baron-Cohen, H. Tager-Flusberg and D.J. Cohen (eds.) *Understanding other minds: Perspectives from developmental cognitive neuroscience.* Oxford: Oxford University Press.

Frith, U. (ed) (1991) *Autism and Asperger Syndrome*. London: Cambridge University Press.

Frith, U. and Happé, F.G.E. (1999) 'Theory of mind and self-consciousness: What is it like to be autistic?' *Mind and Language 14* (1), 1–22.

Gillberg, C. (1984). 'Autistic children growing up: Problems during puberty and adolescence.' *Developmental Medicine and Child Neurosis 26*, 122–129.

Goldstein, G., Johnson, C. and Minshew, N. (2001) 'Attentional processes in Autism'. *Journal of Autism and Developmental Disorders 31*, 4, 433–446.

Grandin, T. (1996) *Thinking in Pictures: And Other Reports from My Life with Autism*. New York: Vintage Books.

Howlin, P. (1997) *Autism: Preparing for Adulthood.* London: Routledge.

Jackson, L. (2003) *Freaks, Geeks and Asperger's Syndrome.* London: Jessica Kingsley Publishers.

Lawson, W. (2000) *Life Behind Glass.* London: Jessica Kingsley Publishers.

Lloyd, S.R. (1988) *Developing Positive Assertiveness: Practical Techniques for Personal Success.* Los Altos, CA: Crisp Publications.

Martin, L. (1990) *Think it – Say it: Improving Reasoning and Organization Skills.* San Antonio, TX: The Psychological Corporation.

McCabe, P., McCabe, E. and McCabe, J. (2002) *Living and Loving with Asperger Syndrome: Family Viewpoints.* London: Jessica Kingsley Publishers.

Morganett, R.S. (1990) *Skills for Living: Group Counselling Activities for Young Adolescents.* Champaign, IL: Research Press.

Murray, D.K.C. (1992) 'Attention tunnelling and autism'. In *Living with Autism: The Individual, the Family and the Professional.* Paper presented at the Durham Conference. Compiled by Autism Research Unit, University of Sunderland, UK. http://osiris.sunderland.ac.uk/autism/confproc.html

Murray, D.K.C. (1995) 'An autistic friendship.' In *Psychological Perspectives in Autism* 183–193. Paper presented at the Durham Conference. Compiled by Autism Research Unit, University of Sunderland, UK. http://osiris.sunderland.ac.uk/autism/confproc.html

Murray, D.K.C. (1996) 'Shared attention and speech in autism.' In *Therapeutic Interventions in Autism.* Paper presented at the Durham Conference. Compiled by Autism Research Unit, University of Sunderland, UK. http://osiris.sunderland.ac.uk/autism/confproc.html

Rodman, K.E. and FAAAS Inc. (2003) *Asperger Syndrome and Adults... Is Anyone Listening? Essays and Poems by Spouses, Partners and Parents of Adults with Asperger Syndrome.* London: Jessica Kingsley Publishers.

Schopler, E. (1995) *Parent Survival Manual: A Guide to Crisis Resolution in Autism.* New York: Plenum Press.

Segar, M. (n.d.) The battles of the autistic thinker. www.autismandcomputing.org.uk/

Sharpley, C., Bitsika, V. and Efremidis, B. (1997) 'The influence of gender, parental health, and perceived expertise of assistance upon the well-being of parents of children with autism.' *Journal of Intellectual and Developmental Disability 22* (1), 19-28.

Slater-Walker, G. and Slater-Walker, C. (2002) *An Asperger Marriage.* London: Jessica Kingsley Publishers.

Stanford, A. (2002) *Asperger Syndrome and Long-Term Relationships.* London: Jessica Kingsley Publishers.

Torisky, D. and Torisky, C. (1985) 'Sex education and sexual awareness building for autistic children and youth: Some viewpoints and consideration.' *Journal of Autism and Developmental Disorders 15,* 2, 213–227.

Willey, L.H. (ed.) (2003) *Asperger Syndrome in Adolescence: Living with the Ups, the Downs and Things in Between.* London: Jessica Kingsley Publishers.

Williams, D. (1998) *Nobody Nowhere.* London: Jessica Kingsley Publishers.

Williams, D. (2004) *Everyday Heaven: Journeys Beyond the Stereotypes of Autism.* London: Jessica Kingsley Publishers.

Wolfensberger, W. (1972) *The Principle of Normalisation in Human Services.* Toronto: National Institute on Mental Retardation.

Subject Index

ASD refers to autistic spectrum disorder, NT to neurotypical; page numbers in italics are tables

abuse 31, 68–70
acceptance
    of ASD by family 93–5
    of differences in
        relationships 103–4
    of self 92, 142
    of sexual orientation
        85–6, 90, 130–1,
        163
activities
    for couples 147–8
    to preserve identity
        outside family 112
adolescence
    development, typical
        versus ASD 90, 91
    difficulties 130
    emotional development,
        delay in ASD 18–19
    sex education for ASD
        36–7
advantages, of ASD 22, 108
affection, personal attitudes
    towards display 15, 132
age of consent 59
alcohol, being in control 58
anxiety 92
    on meeting people 58
appeasement, in relationships
    106
appropriateness
    difficulties with in ASD
        23
    teaching in sex education
        35–6
arguments 113–14
    see also conflict; disputes
ASD: My Gender (poem) 107–8
assessment, for difficulties, at
    university 137
attachment 18, 40
    and empathy 111
    to objects 88–9

see also obsessive
    attachments;
    over-attachment
attitudes
    to gay community 131
    of others towards a
        relationship 49
    positive attitude to past
        122–3
    to public display of
        affection 15, 132
    to sexuality of individuals
        with ASD 31–2, 33
    towards women 82
    to wearing opposite sex
        attire 82
attraction 44
    effect of being attracted
        to someone 52–3
    mutual 54–5
    non-mutual 53
    to someone else when in
        relationship 55
    see also sexual attraction
autistic spectrum disorder
    advantages 22, 108
    disadvantages 13–14
    incidence of
        homosexuality 83,
        144
    worksheet 153–4
autonomy 112–13
    following end of
        relationship 75
    personal autonomy 101,
        102

bad memories 121–3
'baggage' of life 95–6
behaviour management, control
    of environment 38
'being stuck', in an emotion
    50–1
belief systems 100–1, 118
bisexuality 83–4
body language, reading 109
body parts, information in sex
    education 39
building relationships 47, 123

career development, author's
    139–40
change, of individuals with
    ASD, by others 86, 125

child development, in ASD 18
choice, and decision making
    86–7, 105
cleanliness, teaching 38
close-knit families 95–6
closed concepts, thinking style
    23
clothing
    to encourage correct
        behaviour 38
    and gender 81
clubs, for meeting people
    56–7
cognition, worksheet 155
coming out see disclosure
communication 115–20
communication style 116–17
concentration, advantage of
    monotropism 22
concepts, mutual understanding
    in relationships 118–19
confidence, importance in
    relationships 119–20
conflict
    from demands of family
        96
    due to monotropism 65
    due to problems with
        concepts 118–19
    in sexual intimacy 68
    see also arguments;
        disputes
conforming, versus disclosure
    143
control
    through choice and
        decision making
        86–7
    through dealing with past
        122
    of environment to
        manage behaviour 38
    over need for relationship
        48
    over sexual intimacy,
        following abuse 70
conversations, processing
    content of 114, 115–16
couple identity 98–9
couples
    activities for 147–8
    relationships 98–9
    see also partners
courage, in gender issues 87–8

cross-dressing 81–2
crossword puzzles 147, 149, 151
cultural differences, and communication 117

dating 37, 48
    with different sexual orientation 91–2
    inviting a relationship 54–5
    see also meeting people
decision making 86–7
demands
    of families 73–4, 125
    see also expectations
detachment, and emotion 132
developmental approach, to sex education 36–7
developmental delay 18–19
diagnosis, of author's ASD 129
'diffability' 24–5
differences, acceptance in relationships 103–4
diplomacy
    in communication 117
    diplomatic dishonesty by NTs 14, 106
    in relationships 110–11, 141
    see also honesty
disadvantages, of ASD 13–14
disappointment 50
disclosure
    for an improved future 144
    of ASD
        by author 131, 133–4
        in relationship 51–2
    emotional impact and importance 142
    of homosexuality, by author 136
    of thoughts and feelings to others 140–1, 141–2, 143–4
    versus conforming 143
discriminative learning, in sex education 37–8
dishonesty see diplomacy; honesty
disputes 114

see also conflict
distractions, of sensory issues 70–1
divorce 75–6
Doubly Drawn (poem) 84–5
drawing, obsession with objects 88–90

education, author's return as adult 135–8
emotional attachment
    to objects 88–9
    see also attachment; over-attachment
emotional development, delay in ASD 18–19
emotional preference, orientation scale 161
emotions
    in attraction 52–3
    'being stuck' 50–1
    and detachment 132
    difficulties with 29
    identification with 109
empathy 9, 108–10, 111
expectations
    in relationships 64–8, 95, 99
    see also demands
experiences see past experiences

failure 25
falling in love 29–30
families 103
    acceptance of ASD 93–5
    demands of 95–6
    guidance 8, 46, 47, 49
    need for support 77
    prioritizing in 96
family, author's, reaction to disclosure and lifestyle 133–4, 138–9
family types 95–6
fear
    emotion in attraction 52–3
    of sexuality of individuals with ASD 33
feelings
    attraction 52–3
    everyday relationships 72–3
    non-feeling state 132

festive celebrations, demands of families 95–6
first dates 48
flirting 41, 55–6
focusing 13, 22
    in clubs 57
    see also monotropism; single-mindedness
fragrances, problems with 71
freeze framing 50–1
friendships 106
    ability to form 64
    basis for learning about relationships 19, 54
    guidance from 8, 46, 47, 49
    maintaining contact 113

gay relationships see same-sex relationships
gender identity 81, 84, 87–8
generalized learning 22, 23
genetic counselling, and ASD 26
'getting stuck', in an emotion 50–1
grievances, in relationships 97
guidance, by friends and family 8, 46, 47, 49

heterosexuality 63, 162
homosexuality 82–3, 85–6, 162
    see also bisexuality; same-sex relationships
honesty 110
    see also diplomacy

'I' pronoun, in conversation 117
identity
    in couples relationship 100
    preserving in family life 111–12
    see also image; sense of self; sexual identity
image 92, 101, 103, 116
    see also identity; sense of self
incidence, of homosexuality and ASD 83, 144
information, about function of body parts 39

information processing,
needing time 114
intellectual disability, and ASD
25–7
Internet 92, 113
interpersonal skills, teaching
37
IQ 25–6

jewellery, problems in sexual
intimacy 71
Joan and Bob (poem) 94–5

Kinsey Scale for Sexual
Orientation 159, 162
Klein Sexual Orientation Grid
159–63
Knowing You, Knowing Me
(poem) 120

language 26, 156
learning difficulties 25
assessment at university
137–8
rights 20
learning styles 21–4
lesbian relationships *see*
same-sex relationships
Life Behind Glass
(autobiography) 140
lifestyle, orientation scale 162
listening, in relationships 65
literality 22–3, 67
love 28–9
being in love 66

marriage
of author 130–1
success 60
marriage guidance 76
masturbation 59, 60
appropriate places 23, 38
attitude towards
individuals with ASD
31
medication, before and after
diagnosis 134–5
meeting people 55–8, 91–2
see also dating
memories *see* bad memories
minority status, of homosexual
individuals with ASD 83
monotropism 13

and adolescence 130
and effect of attraction to
someone 53
and empathy 109
and falling in love
29–30
and gender issues 88
learning style 22–4
effect on relationships
46, 65
worksheets 156, 157
see also focusing;
single-mindedness
mother, author's, reaction to
disclosure and lifestyle
134, 139
moving on, from past 121–3
mutual attraction 53, 54–5
My Body (poem) 17
My Love (poem) 65–6

natural responses 40
see also normality
needs
author's, accommodation
of at university
137–8
of partner 64–5, 67, 96
in relationships 67–8
sexual intimacy 68
negative experiences *see* past
experiences
nervousness, when meeting
people 58
neuro-typical individuals *see*
NTs
nightclubs 56–7
non-generalized learning, in
monotropism 23
non-literality 21
non-social priorities, in
monotropism 23
normality 24, 40
NTs (neuro-typical individuals)
ability to read body
language and signs
109
characteristics 14–15
diplomatic dishonesty
14, 106
single status 64

objects, emotional attachment
88–9

obsessive attachments 40, 46,
129–30
see also attachment
one-night stands 57–8
open concepts, thinking style
21
'other'
difficulties in adjusting to
29
noticing others 41
separation from 46
understanding concept
22, 24
outcomes
of disclosure 138–44
prediction 22, 24
over-attachment 40, 46,
129–30
see also attachment

parenting 76–7
parents, relationship with
children 45
partners
in couple relationship
98–9
needs 64–5, 67, 96
see also other; relationships
past experiences 121–3, 140
personal autonomy 101, 102
personal columns, for meeting
people 57
personal hygiene, teaching 38
poems 17, 43, 65, 94–5, 102,
107–8, 120, 126
polytropism, learning style
21–2
positive image
of self 92
see also image; self-image
prediction of outcomes 22, 24
promiscuity, disappointment of
84
puberty *see* adolescence
pubs, for meeting people 56–7

questions, to establish
responsibility 47

readiness, for relationships 49
reassurance, in relationships 67
rebuilding relationships 123

recreation 103
    away from family 74
    in retirement 112–13
rejection 50–1
    of author at school 137
relationship counselling 76
relationships
    acceptance
        of differences
            103–4
        the real person 72
    areas for consideration
        44
    attitudes of others
        towards 49
    attraction 52–5
        to someone else 55
    being prepared for ups
        and downs 66
    change 74–5
    coping with rejection
        50–1
    couples 98–9
    dealing with disputes
        114
    difficulties
        with emotions 29
        in puberty 18–19
    diplomatic dishonesty
        110–11
    drawbacks of ASD
        13–14
    empathy 108–10
    endings 75
    everyday feelings 72–3
    everyday problems 45–6
    expectations in 64–8,
        95, 99
    growth 101–2
    importance of confidence
        119–20
    learning to relate 48
    loss of sense of self 73
    negative relationships,
        effects 45
    NT rules and expectations
        15
    positive aspects of 60
    purpose 45–6
    re-evaluating 97
    rebuilding after negative
        experiences 123
    responsibility in 47, 99
    as a safe place 105–7

and sex 58–61, 68–72
and sharing 110, 125–7
time for development 57
see also partners; romantic
    relationships
Relationships (poem) 43
relaxation 103
reliability, of individuals with
    ASD 14
responsibility
    in relationships 47, 99
    effect of terminology 27
retarded, use of term 27
retirement, effect on identity
    112–13
revisiting experiences 140
rights
    expectations disguised as
        95
    of learning disabled 20
role models 49–50
role-play 40–1
romantic relationships 19, 47,
    63–4
    see also relationships
routines, recognising
    importance of 97
rudeness, resulting from
    monotropism 22
rules see unspoken rules

safe places, in relationships
    105–7
same-sex relationships 63
    affection 39–40
    see also bisexuality;
        homosexuality
saying 'no' to sex 60–1
scents, problems with 71
school, author's experiences as
    adult 135
self-confidence 92
    through disclosure
        142–3
self-esteem, effect of negative
    self-esteem 116
self-identification, orientation
    scale 162
self-image 92, 101, 103, 116
sense of self 112
    loss in demanding
        relationships 73
    maintaining 125

see also identity; image;
    self-image
sensory overload 70–1
sensory profile, discussion sheet
    165–6
separation, at end of
    relationship 75
separation anxiety 73
sex, and relationships 58–61
sex education
    concerns over 33
    levels of learning 37–9
    need for 7
    providers 39
    related to developmental
        stage 34
    systematic approach
        35–6
sexual abuse 31, 68–70
sexual arousal 28
sexual attraction
    orientation scale 161
    see also attraction
sexual behaviour
    orientation scale 161
    teaching appropriateness
        35–6
sexual desire 59, 132
sexual fantasies, orientation
    scale 161
sexual identity
    fluidity 163
    see also bisexuality;
        homosexuality;
        identity; same-sex
        relationships; sexual
        orientation
sexual intimacy 68, 70–2
sexual orientation
    acceptance 85–6, 90
        by author 130–1,
            133
    worksheet 159–63
    see also bisexuality;
        homosexuality;
        same-sex relationships
sexuality
    in ASD 27–8
    definition 19–20
    developmental tasks 32
    negative attitude towards
        ASD 31, 32–3
    personal attitudes 16

rights of adults with
    learning disabilities
    20
and trust, worksheet 158
sharing, in relationships 46,
    110, 125–7
signs
    appropriate places for
        sexual behaviour 38
    reading other people
        109
single-mindedness 14, 25
    see also focusing;
        monotropism
single parenting 76–7
single status 63–4
smiling, signals 54
social preference, orientation
    scale 161–2
social priorities 21, 23
social relationships, difficulties
    in puberty 18–19
social understanding 8
socialization, and
    monotropism, worksheet
    157
solitude, need for 74
spatial ability, in NTs 22
spoken language 26, 156
    see also verbal ability
statistical incidence, of
    homosexuality and ASD
    83, 144
stress 92
    see also anxiety
support
    for developing sexuality
        33
    in difficulties 124–5
    for families 77
    and sexual orientation
        163
support groups, run by author
    for parents of ASD
    children 139

talking
    about the relationship and
        sex 61
    balance between partners
        71
television
    portrayal of family life
        132–3

watching drama to
    understand flirting
    56
terminology, effect on
    responsibility 27
'theory of mind' 22, 24
thinking 21, 23
time
    concept of 14, 22
    need for in processing
        information 114,
        115–16
    for solitude 74
Time (poem) 126
touch 68, 70
The Tree of Life (poem) 102
trust, and sexuality worksheet
    158
truthfulness see diplomacy;
    honesty
turn-ons 71–2

underage sex 59–60, 72
understanding other people
    108–10
university, experiences of
    author 136–8
unspoken rules, problems for
    individuals with ASD 15

verbal ability
    lack of 26
    and sex education 36
vicarious living 46
voices, problems with volume
    and tone 70

whole picture, not
    understanding 23
word searches 147, 150, 152

Author Index

AIHW 131
Allen, W. 84
Anxiety Disorders Association
    of America 92
Asperger, H. 24
Australian Bureau of Statistics
    92
Australian Institute of Health
    and Welfare 131

Carol, L. 92
Croft, A. 20

Gillberg, C. 31

Hamilton, A. 162, 163

Keppel, B. 162, 163
Kinsey, A.C. 159, 162
Klein, F. 159–63

Lawson, W. 21, 33
Loefler, I. 82

Martin, C.E. 159
Mesibov, G.B. 18, 32, 33, 34
Mortlock, J. 20
Moxon, L. 18, 19
Murray, D.K.C. 21, 28–30, 66

Newport, J. 44
Newport, M. 44

Pomeroy, W.B. 159
Pukki, H. 7, 32, 88

Reber, S. 155, 156, 157

Schopler, E. 18, 32, 33
Segar, M. 44
Sepekoff, B. 162

TEACCH 37
Treatment and Education of
    Autistic and Related
    Communication
    Handicapped Children
    (TEACCH) 37
Wolf, T.J. 162